Contents

Appendices

Introduction

As ever, in education, we are going through a period of radical curriculum change plus changes in the assessment regime. The onus will no longer be on Year 2 and Year 6 teachers to carry the key responsibility for standards in a school. Every year will become more accountable. More significantly, getting children to a benchmark standard or level of achievement will no longer be sufficient; schools must be able to demonstrate the *progress* made by their pupils, from whatever their starting point. OFSTED will be looking for evidence of every child making progress in every year group and teachers will be expected to know where each child is and what is being done to help their progression. Such tracking and identification of next steps is at the heart of *Big Writing*.

Increasingly, the authorities and those in government are recognising the importance of talk in education and the serious impact of language deprivation on standards in tests and examinations. In *Big Writing* we have been saying 'If the child can't say it, the child can't write it,' since 1997. That is why the whole philosophy of *Big Writing* is rooted in teaching children to write better through talk.

This new publication, now fully updated to reflect the demands of the 2014 curriculum in England, has been written as a practical guide on how to plan and teach Big Writing in the classroom. It is aimed at the class teacher or English leader who has identified a need to raise writing standards. It is suggested that teachers implement *Big Writing*, as it is described here, for at least a half term before adapting the model to suit their own teaching style. The basic structure should, however, remain true to the approach.

This handbook includes six lesson plans to enable the teacher to start with confidence, although use of the plans and associated resources is optional.

In order to teach *Big Writing* effectively, the teacher will need:

- full understanding of the process – as outlined in this book
- firm belief in its power to work
- a sense of humour
- a positive approach
- high expectations for all children's achievement
- masses of energy.

> **"... the whole philosophy of *Big Writing* is rooted in teaching children to write better through talk."**

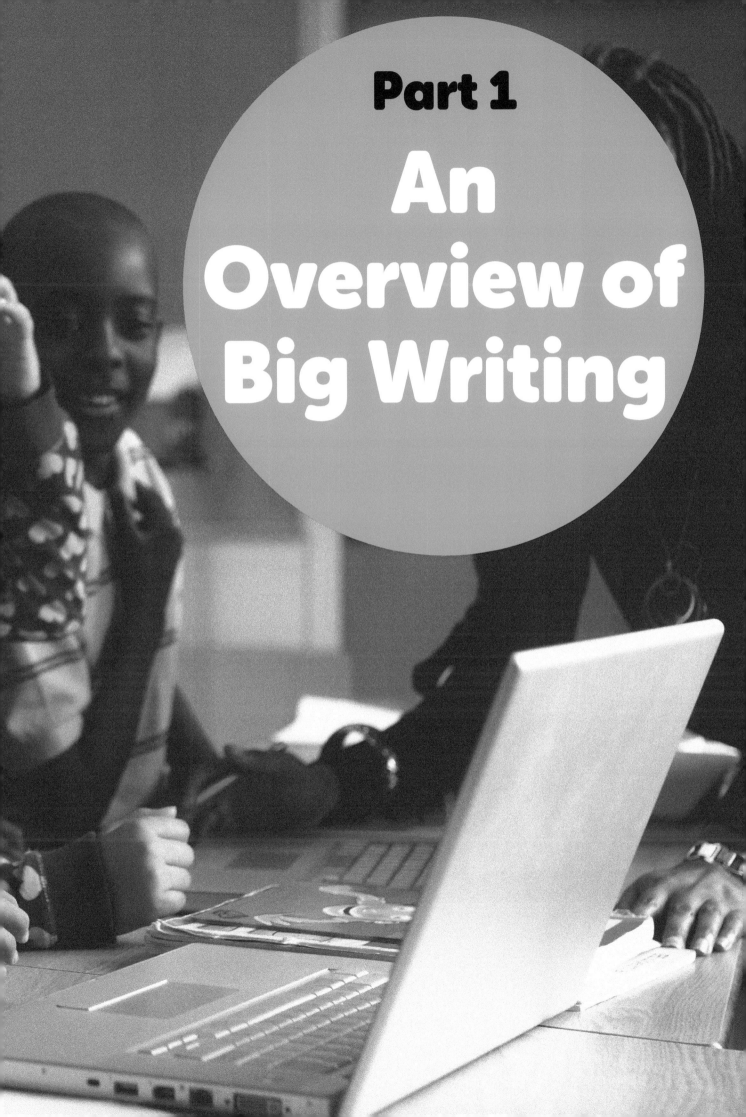

Part 1

An Overview of Big Writing

01: An Overview of Big Writing

WHAT IS BIG WRITING?

Big Writing is an approach to teaching writing and raising writing standards that focuses on:

- The importance of TALK and oral rehearsal

- Accurate basic skills – spelling, punctuation, grammar, handwriting

- Meaningful, termly summative and formative assessment using the Writing Criterion Scale to check progress and inform the next learning steps needed

- High expectations for all pupils

- Giving writing a purpose and making it fun!

The Writer's Toolkit

In *Big Writing,* the full range of writing skills is called the **Writer's Toolkit** and can be summarised as 'The Two WHATS and the Two HOWS':

WHAT 1:   The text type or genre to be written

WHAT 2:   The stimulus or purpose for writing

HOW 1:   Basic Skills: GHaSP

HOW 2:   'Writing Voice'

Most schools are now confident in teaching the two WHATs. *Big Writing* provides schools with a framework for teaching the two HOWs through lively, fun, focused activities and a weekly opportunity for children to apply their skills in an extended writing task.

The four **basic skills** that children need to draw on with increasing automaticity and fluency in their writing are:

- **Grammar** – the use of correct grammar/standard English at all times.

- **Handwriting** – accurate, fast and flowing, preferably using a cursive style.

At a minimum, neat and legible.

- **Spelling** – accurate in all sight words and the majority of ambitious vocabulary, and demonstrating the full range of phonic strategies.

- **Punctuation** – accurate use of all sentence punctuation and creative but accurate use of a wide range of punctuation for 'voice' and effect.

The writer's voice defines both the language the writer uses and the style with which he or she structures sentences. In *Big Writing* it is taught through VCOP, which is:

- The range of **vocabulary** the child has and can use, including ambitious vocabulary (also known as Wow Words).

- The use of a wide range of **connectives**, including more sophisticated connectives.

- The range of ways the child has for **opening** sentences, including the use of the three Power Openers (connectives, 'ly' words and 'ing' words).

- The range of **punctuation** the child uses, including punctuation for effect or Power Punctuation (? ! ...)

Big Writing therefore consists of:

- **Daily basic skills:** 10 minutes every day covering phonics, spelling and handwriting

- **Stocking fillers:** short, 5 minute VCOP sessions to recycle skills from the previous week

- **'Bells' work:** quick-fire 'make me up ...' activities to embed new language and skills whilst waiting for playtime, lunch, etc

- **The Big Write:** extended VCOP session followed by an extended, silent writing session.

The **Big Write** session consists of:

- A 'talk' homework the night before – for children to discuss and prepare (mentally) what they are going to write about.

- One hour per week in Year 1, split into two 30 minute sessions: one before and one after morning playtime. It may be introduced as 10 minutes and 10 minutes initially and built up to the full 30/30.

- One and a half hours in Years 2 to 6, split into two 45 minute sessions: one before and one after morning playtime. In Year 2, it may start with two 30 minute sessions and gradually increase to 45/45.

- First 35 minutes = fast, fun work on correct use of vocabulary, connectives, sentence openers and punctuation (VCOP).

- Followed by 10 minutes of planning time.

- After play the children write individually, in silence, with an atmosphere that supports both concentration and creativity (dimmed lights, low volume Mozart, regular brain breaks).

Assessment and the Oxford Writing Criterion Scale

The **Oxford Writing Criterion Scale** – provided in full in Appendix 1 – is at the heart of the *Big Writing* approach. It is a generic scale, divided in to a series of Standards, that supports the accurate assessment of writing in line with national expectations and provides detailed identification of the specific skills children need to improve in order to make progress.

Big Writing is all about involving pupils in their learning by sharing the 'secret garden' of assessment with them. By explaining exactly what we're doing in terms of assessment and setting clear, manageable targets, we can excite and empower pupils to make progress. This approach is particularly helpful in motivating children who are already disaffected by writing – especially boys.

As well as regular assessment for learning, the *Big Writing* approach recommends monitoring children's progress based on three formal summative assessments each school year from Years 1 to 6. During these **Targeted Assessment Tasks** (or TATs), pupils are required to produce a piece of unsupported writing within a timed period. Each piece should be assessed using the Oxford Writing Criterion Scale and awarded a Standard. It is still useful to sub-divide each Standard into three parts, which we label developing, secure and advanced, to enable more specific tracking, recognition of progress within a Standard and more specific target setting. The child should then be set a long-term target for achievement over a specific period (e.g. by the time of the next TAT) and three short-term 'small steps' targets to support immediate progress towards the long-term target.

Further details on the *Big Writing* approach to assessment can be found in *Raising Writing Standards: A powerful and effective whole-school approach* by Ros Wilson (OUP, 2012).

The Big Writing Toolkit

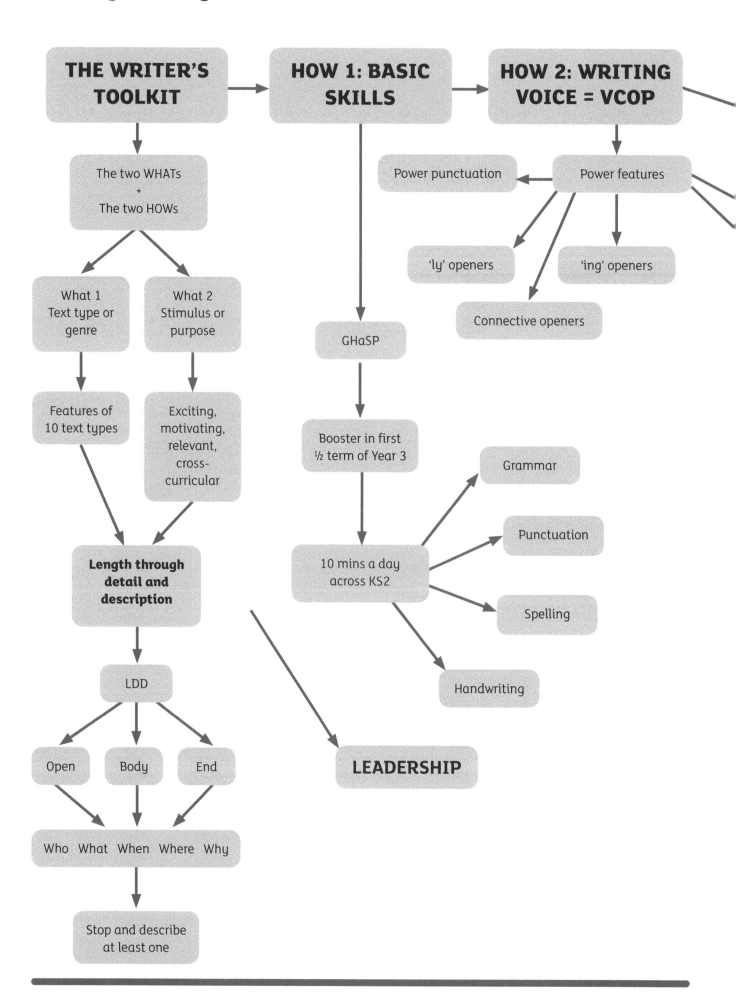

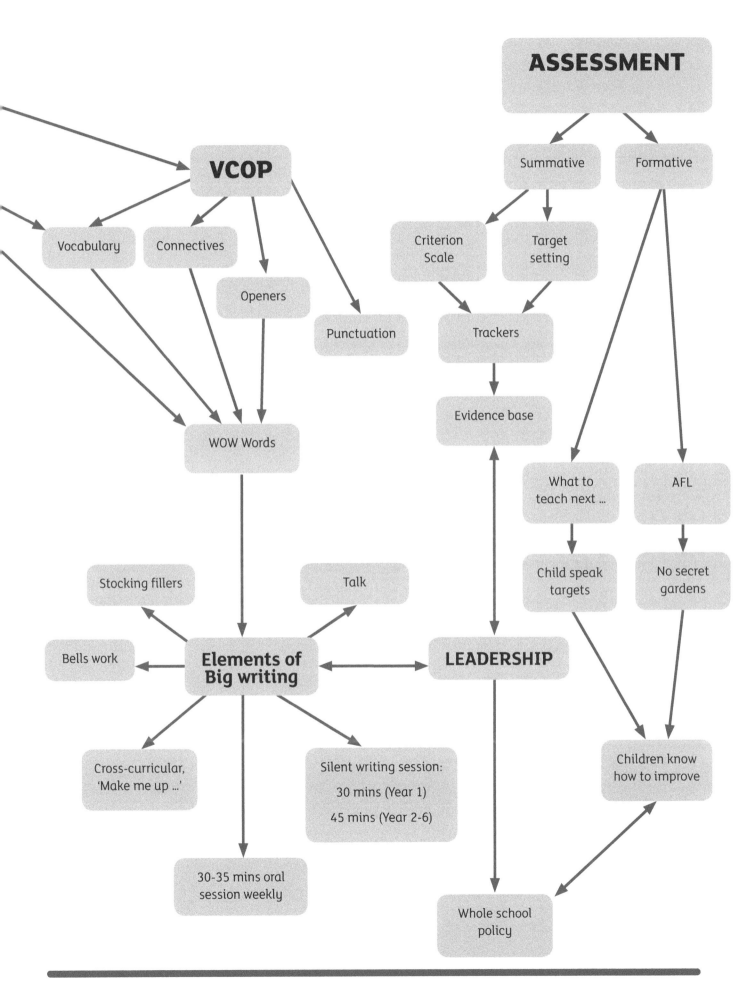

The Big Writing Action Plan

The Action Plan below is designed to help you get started with *Big Writing*. Ideas for implementing the Action Plan, including practical activities and lesson plans, are provided in Part 2 of this book.

1	BASELINE ASSESS	Use the Oxford Writing Criterion Scale (see *Appendix 1*) to assess a piece of unsupported writing from every child **before** the first Big Write Session.
2	BUY or SOURCE MATERIALS	Source the materials you will need for the Big Write session and for the Class Evidence Base: • Candle or lava lamp • Classical music • Special pens and paper • Food treats as rewards • Class folder for assessments
3	PREPARE EVIDENCE BASE	Create a folder in which to store the assessment record for the whole class and the three annual Targeted Assessment Tasks for each pupil.
4	IDENTIFY TIMETABLE TIME	The Big Write session requires two slots of 30 minutes each in Year 1, rising to 45 minutes each in Year 2 and beyond. Plan this double session straddling morning playtime, preferably on a Thursday or Friday.
5.	PLAN TEXT TYPE AND STIMULUS	The text type and stimulus for the Big Write session should be linked to on-going work in English and/or linked to the wider curriculum. Make sure it is interesting / stimulating.
6	PLAN LIVELY VCOP SESSION	Plan a series of fun activities (called 'games') that move constantly back and forth across all aspects and levels of VCOP.
7	BRIEFLY REVIEW TEXT TYPE THE AFTERNOON BEFORE	Remind children when they learned the text to be written and spend up to 10 minutes on a quick review (visual and oral) of its features. The text type should always be one that has already been learnt.
8	GIVE TALK HOMEWORK (STIMULUS) THE DAY BEFORE	Prepare the slips to send home, informing families what the topic for talk is. Go over the stimulus for 5 minutes.
9	TEACH ORAL SESSION – LIVELY AND FUN!	Open the first session with 35 minutes (25 in Year 1) of lively, fun VCOP activities and games. Spend 5-10 minutes on quiet planning.
10	PREPARE THE ENVIRONMENT AT PLAYTIME	Prepare the classroom environment for the Big Write session. Dim the lights and light a candle or lava lamp. Play classical music softly.
11	MANAGE THE SILENT WRITING SESSION	Meet the children at the door and ensure they come in in silence, sit in silence and start to write. Then sit and model self as a writer, speaking only for the time prompts.
12	MARK THE WRITING CAREFULLY	Praise at least three positives from stimulus and voice. Give two targets for progress in the next week.
13	RETURN THE WRITING PROMPTLY	Return writing as soon as possible – the following day, or the following Monday. Give up to 15 minutes for children to read the comments together, in pairs, and discuss the targets, to identify what they did well.
14	PLAN FURTHER TEACHING	Use progress observed during the oral session and while marking to identify areas for teaching during the stocking filler sessions and the next oral session.

1 Baseline assess

- Assess a piece of unsupported writing using the Oxford Writing Criterion Scale (see *Appendix 1*).

- Create a spread sheet or table with every child's name down the side and several columns.

- Put the child's date of birth in the second column.

- Put the child's first language, if not English, in the third column.

- Put the date of the baseline assessment at the top of the fourth column and enter the Standards.

- Set a target for where the child should be by the end of the academic year in the fifth column.

- Put the date for the next assessment in the top of the next column.

2 Buy or source materials

- Buy special pens for *Big Writing*, if you can afford them.

- Decide where children will do the writing – ring binder, folder, special book?

- Organise a CD player and classical music (preferably Mozart).

- Buy a real or electric large candle or a lava lamp.

- Buy some treats to use as rewards during the Big Write session – grapes, tangerines, sweets or chocolates.

- Have a large, easy-to-read clock hung above the whiteboard.

- Source materials for the class Evidence Base – a regular ring binder, plastic pockets, sticky labels.

3 Prepare evidence base

- Put every child's name, date of birth and first language, if other than English, onto a label and attach one to each plastic pocket.

- Put the spread sheet created for the Baseline Assessment into the first plastic pocket in the ring binder.

- Put the first baseline assessed piece of writing into each child's plastic pocket, turned backwards. Each subsequent piece is then inserted facing the right way. This enables a visual comparison of progress to be made instantly.

4 Identify timetable time

- Identify the day of the week that is to contain the Big Write session, preferably on a Thursday or Friday.

- Adjust the timetable for that day to allow the Big Write session of 1½ hours (1 hour in Year 1) to be split exactly in half by morning playtime, creating two 45 minute sessions (two 30 minute sessions in Year 1).

- Allow an additional 10-15 minutes that day for children to read, edit and improve their work.

For advice on using *Big Writing* in the Foundation Stage see page 40, or refer to *Talk the Big Talk: Building the foundations for Big Writing and beyond,* by Ros Wilson, (OUP, 2012).

5 Plan the text type and stimulus

- Plan the text type to be written in the second part of the Big Write session.

- Ensure the text type is one that the children have already experienced in the school's teaching sequence for text types.

- Select an exciting stimulus for the children to write to.

- Whenever possible, ensure the text type, stimulus and purpose for writing springs out of learning in the wider curriculum. Thus, if the children are writing a historical report, the 45 minutes writing time comes from the history timetable.

6 Plan a lively VCOP session

- Plan a range of fast, fun VCOP activities or 'games' for the 35 minute oral session (*see pages 18-23*). Plan for 20 to 25 minutes in Year 1.

- Ensure the games and activities move backwards and forwards across the four elements of VCOP and across all levels of VCOP.

7 Briefly review the text type

- Tell the children what text type they will be writing in the Big Write session the next day.

- Relate it to an aspect of their learning that week.

- Remind them when they last wrote this text (*see page 24*).

- Refresh their memories of how to write the text type.

- Show examples of the text if necessary.

- Place examples of the text round the classroom for them to study if they want to.

- Put the poster with the features of the text type up (if it isn't already), for them to study if they wish.

- Point out where they can find an example of the text type in their previous work, if they wish to look at it.

8 Give the Talk Homework

- Give children a pre-prepared Talk Homework slip to take home, telling their parents/carers what they are going to be writing about (*'stimulus' see pages 23-24*).

- Relate the stimulus to recent learning in a subject of the curriculum.

- Encourage a brief discussion of preliminary ideas for what to write about.

9 Teach the Big Write oral session, making it lively and fun!

- 35 minutes of fast, fun, lively VCOP activities (*see pages 18-23*); 25 minutes in Year 1.

- Move backwards and forwards across the elements of VCOP and the levels of VCOP.

- Note carefully the confidence and accuracy with which all children are responding.

- Adjust the balance and levels to ensure all children are achieving.

- Revisit a particular activity if necessary.

- Note any activities that should be repeated as Stocking Fillers the next week (*see page 27*).

- Allow up to 10 minutes for children to plan their writing. Children choose how to plan their writing. (*See Appendix 3 – Planning for Writing – which should be taught in Year 1.*)

10 Prepare the environment for the Big Write silent writing

- Choose two children (on a rota basis) to help you set up the classroom.

- The children should put the writing paper or book, special pen and food rewards in each child's place on the tables.

- The teacher starts the Mozart music, turning it so low that it can barely be heard unless the room is totally silent.

- The teacher reduces the lighting by closing the blinds, turning off lights, lighting a candle or lava lamp, or similar action.

- The teacher stands by the door to manage the silent entry of the class.

11 Manage the silent writing session

- The children walk in silence to their places, sit down and start to write.

- The teacher waits a few minutes to ensure all have started confidently.

- The teacher sits down at a table and starts to write.

- The teacher only breaks the silence to point to the clock and give the time prompts (*pages 25-26*).

- The teacher should emphasise the need to finish off at the final 'Five minutes left' time prompt.

- The writing is collected in for marking.

12 Mark the writing carefully

- Mark the writing by identifying at least three strengths in the margin with a small line under the exact bit.

- Identify up to three areas for editing or development, in the margin, with a small underline below the item it refers to.

- At the bottom, write what they have done well and two areas for development.

- Comment on Basic Skills (*see pages 33-36*).

- Make a note to yourself of any teaching points needed.

13 Return the writing promptly

- Return the writing the following day or as soon as possible

- Identify a 10 to 15 minute slot for return of the writing and expect the children to read the feedback in pairs and talk about what you have said. Mixed ability pairings make this easier.

- Support any pairs you feel may find this hard.

- Give a general summary of overall performance and read a positive example. Ensure that all children have an excerpt read out at some point.

14 Plan the next oral session and stocking fillers

- Use your observations from the oral VCOP session and marking of the children's work to identify areas that require further teaching.

- Adapt any activities identified for repetition as 'Stocking Fillers' by making small changes to keep them fresh.

- Identify which activities should be repeated or extended in the next Big Write oral session.

- Mix repeated activities and games with new examples for the next oral session.

Part 2

Implementing the Big Writing Action Plan

02: Implementing the Big Writing Action Plan

BRINGING BIG WRITING TO LIFE

Over the following pages you will find a range of fun, practical ideas and activities to help you deliver the *Big Writing* approach in the classroom. All of these ideas can be adapted to suit the needs of your children and your own teaching style, and it can be useful to share and swap ideas with colleagues. The important thing is to keep the teaching focused, fresh, lively and enjoyable for everyone.

What might be included in the range of fast, fun VCOP activities?

1 'Up-Levelling'

Display a piece of writing – created by yourself or the 'imaginary friend' (see below) – and work with pupils to raise the standard of the text through:

- Inserting describing words (adjectives and adverbs).

- Changing connectives into more sophisticated connectives – for example, 'but' becomes 'however'.

- Changing nouns, verbs, adjectives and adverbs into 'WOW' words, for example, 'bowl' becomes 'receptacle' or 'vessel'; 'says' becomes 'announces' or 'enunciates'; 'old' becomes 'ancient' or 'dilapidated'; 'quickly' becomes 'swiftly' or 'rapidly' and so on.
  NB Ensure children know and understand the meaning of all ambitious vocabulary and use the words appropriately in the text.

- Re-structuring sentences by creating a Power Opener, inserting a question or direct speech, or inserting brackets or an embedded clause using 'The Two Comma Trick', for example: *The man ran, clutching the injured dog in his arms, up to the door of the vet's house.*

2 'Big It Up'

Often known as 'Big It Up Monday', this activity builds on the historic teaching strategy of talking about children's 'news' on a Monday morning. Prior to the National Curriculum, the first session of Monday morning was often spent by children talking and then writing their 'news' from the weekend.

In a 'Big It Up' session, children are encouraged to invent things that did not really happen at the weekend, but that they would have loved to happen! These could include things such as:

- The Queen stopped by to use the loo...

- I found a million pounds in my...

- The Tooth Fairy brought me...

- I found a bottle that contained a magic genie who...

- I was performing in *Britain's Got Talent* when...

This technique can then be used at random times in the week to promote talk and the development of children's imaginative powers.

3 Spot the Difference

Give children two passages of the same text written at two different Standards (usually Standards 4 and 6) – either as hard copy or displayed electronically.

- Explain that the two pieces tell the same story or report the same event, but at very different Standards.

- The Standard 4 text is technically accurate but 'deadly boring' and the Standard 6 text is the 'all whistles and bells' passage.

- Children talk and use highlighters to identify the features that make the second piece a higher Standard.

- This will usually be through identifying aspects of VCOP, but could be varied by the first passage having low Basic Skills and the second passage being totally accurate – to emphasise the importance of good basic skills in achieving a high standard in writing.

4 Steal!

Stealing can happen in all subjects at random times throughout the week, but with planned opportunities in English lessons.

- Whenever a teacher uses text with pupils (whether as a source for learning or as literature for pleasure) every opportunity is taken to 'steal' new words or language.

- This is not a passive activity. The teacher 'activates' pupils' learning by saying things like: "Just before I / we read this passage / page there is a fantastic new 'WOW' word / 'Power Opener' / use of _____ here, see if you can spot it."

- The new word or phrase is then written on card and displayed on the wall and becomes the focus for Bells Work ('Make me up ...') and, when appropriate, stocking fillers and games in the oral session.

5 Teach the Imaginary Friend

'The Imaginary Friend' is a challenging concept for some teachers. A teacher needs to lose his/her inhibitions and be willing to trust the class in order to introduce this concept but it can be extremely powerful. The Imaginary Friend is also a source of humour, which is a key element of Big Writing.

The imaginary friend is treated as a 'real' pupil who does not exist. He is:

- Male, because he doubles as a role model for the boys.

- Gifted, in that he can answer the questions nobody else can answer, including the quick questions, thus avoiding the need to wait while children 'fumble' the way to an answer.

- 'Low ability' in that he makes and owns all the mistakes which pupils in the class make, so that they are not embarrassed by having their errors used in teaching.

The Imaginary Friend should be given a name, preferably a really obscure or old-fashioned name that should never arrive in the school as a genuine name – Marmaduke is a popular one!

When the children make mistakes, the imaginary friend makes them too and the teacher brings 'his' work to the class, either as hard copy or displayed electronically, so that the class can 'teach' him how to correct the error and thus learn themselves.

Then, when the children write, the teacher can remind them not to make the same mistakes that '_____' made. The mistakes include things the children do in error such as:

- Spelling errors

- Grammar errors

- Missing punctuation

- Miss-use of punctuation

- Miss-use of 'WOW' words

- Missing capital letters

- Illegible handwriting

- Use of simple language only

Unfinished work from the imaginary friend is used to teach children ways to finish off work when given the '5 minutes to finish' warning in the Big Write session.

6 Guesstimate Standard

Children from age 7 should learn to identify 'by sight' the broad Standard of a piece of writing. It is better to use pieces of writing that are secure at a Standard.

Children should be taught to be able to 'guesstimate' a Standard and justify their decisions based on the characteristics of the piece. To this end, a broad description of the characteristics of each Standard is provided on pages 28-29.

7 Put in sequence by Standard

Children should be taught to put pieces of writing in an approximate sequence of Standards and should be able to justify the ordering.

8 Bells Work or 'Make me up...'

In every spare moment, including those moments when the class has tidied up and is waiting for the bell to ring for assembly, for play time, for lunch, for the hall for P.E. or in similar situations, teachers should take a few moments to ask children to make up sentences (orally) that include current teaching points such as:

- 'WOW' words
- Power Openers
- Power Features
- Power Punctuation
- The range of punctuation.

9 Snappy Synonyms

This can be played with no expense through the following:

1 Teacher posts a word on the whiteboard, for example, 'pretty'.

2 Teacher counts backwards from 10 to 1 (or uses some time device).

3 Children brainstorm three or more words that could be used instead, for example, 'beautiful', 'attractive', 'delectable'.

4 Synonyms agreed OR go to dictionary game OR the thesaurus game.

Antonym Games can also be played in the same way as 'Snappy Synonyms'.

10 Dictionary and Thesaurus Games

- The teacher counts back from 10 to 1 (or uses another timing device) while children locate a given word in the dictionary and read out the definition.
- The teacher counts back from 10 to 1 (or uses another timing device) while children locate a word in the thesaurus and read out the synonyms.

11 Call My Bluff

This game requires no investment other than planning time and is played as follows:

1 Teacher posts a true 'WOW' word on the whiteboard.

2 Teacher posts three potential definitions for the 'WOW' word on the white board, each definition labelled by a letter or number.

3 Children opt by shouting or writing down the letter or number for the answer they think is right.

4 Teacher posts the correct answer.

5 Play 'Make me up...' as in Bells Work above.

12 Connective/Opener/ WOW Word Games

These can be used for Bells Work or 'Make me up...' Children become quick and confident in making up oral sentences that start with or include:

- A connective sentence opener, e.g. 'When...' 'If...' 'Because...' 'Although...' Despite....' 'In spite of...' As well as...' 'Contrary to...' 'In addition to...' 'Besides...'

- Other Power Openers such as 'ly' words e.g. 'Slowly...' 'Quickly...' Happily...' 'Unfortunately...' 'Desperately...' 'Impatiently...'

- Other Power Openers such as 'ing' words e.g. 'Walking...' 'Hoping...' Thinking...' 'Anticipating...' Cogitating...'

- A 'WOW' word, e.g. Intrepid, Audacious, Tenacious, Insidious, Abrasive, Loquacious, Ferocious, Pretentious, Contagious, Degrading, Contemplating, Anticipating, Hoping, Reflecting.

Whenever the teacher uses the term 'ly' word they should always add the term 'adverb'; when they use the term 'ing' word they should add the term 'participle'; whenever they use the term 'describing word' they should add 'adjective or adverb'.

13 Loop Games

Teachers can EITHER use commercially produced Loop Games such as those from www.andrelleducation.co.uk OR make up their own by:

1 Making a list of true 'WOW' words.

2 Making playing cards, each with a 'WOW' word definition on, for example, 'I am an evil, spiteful person.'

3 Making the opposite card with the 'WOW' word on, 'I am **malevolent**'.

4 Under the 'WOW' word, write a different definition, for example, 'I am very sweet and good to eat or look at.'

5 The child with the 'start' card reads the first definition and the one with the 'WOW' word answer shouts it out, then reads the definition on their own card.

6 The game continues until all cards have been read out.

14 Power Talk Pictures

Teachers use the internet or similar to find exciting or controversial pictures to promote talk and discussion. Use unusual or provocative pictures to pose questions such as:

- How could this happen?

- How might this have happened?

- What might have caused this?

- What might be about to happen?

- What could be the outcome of this?

- Who might have seen this?

- What would you do if this happened to you?

- What might he be saying?

- What might she be thinking?

15 Purple Balls

Teachers can buy inflatable purple balls from www.andrelleducation.co.uk OR buy any inflatable 'beach ball', and a silver or tippex pen. Then:

1 Write a 'WOW' word or 'POWER OPENER' on each 'face' of the inflatable ball.

2 Put a ball on each table in the class.

3 Ask children to make up games that use the ball.

4 Ask children to throw the ball to a random group member.

5 When a child catches the ball, they make up a sentence that includes ... (the WOW word or Power Opener closest to the child's pointing finger or thumb).

16 Punctuation Games

Play games with punctuation such as shouting sentences at the class that require different pieces of punctuation at the end. Children respond by shouting and drawing (by finger in the air to the left, or on the table, or on the left sleeve) to show the punctuation that should go at the end of the sentence. In addition children can take part in Kung Fu Punctuation games, learned from the *VCOP Games CD ROM* available from www.andrelleducation.co.uk. (*See also pages 106-107.*)

17 Scrambled words

Post up a 'WOW' word (whether noun, adjective, verb, adverb or connective) with the letters muddled. Tell the children which word class it is and ask them to 'sort it out' into the correct form, for example: 'Belcatedel' = 'Delectable'. This would usually be a 'WOW' word currently under focus in Bells Work.

18 Scrambled sentences

Power Sentences are put on the whiteboard OR on card with the words in the wrong order and children have to sort the words into the right order so that the sentence makes sense. For example: 'John lost was unfortunately woods in spooky.' = 'Unfortunately John was lost in the spooky woods.'

Sentences such as this might be unscrambled at a 'lower' level, but can then be re-formed into the highest potential level. For example, the above sentence might have firstly been unscrambled as, 'John was lost in the spooky woods, unfortunately.' The initial letter may be given as a clue.

19 How many true words made from a WOW word?

Give a 'WOW' word that you want children to learn and ask them to find as many true words within it that they can. For example, in **Supercilious** you can find:

- Super
- Sup
- Sip
- Cup
- Cope
- Crisis
- less
- sure
- cross
- pole
- rule
- rope

20 WOW Word Searches

These can be done in a variety of ways including:

- Reading and stealing from texts
- Stealing from passages in 'Spot The Difference'.
- Dictionary Skills
- Thesaurus Skills

21 Fastest Finger First

Usually used in 'Spot the Difference' or 'Up-Levelling' where the teacher poses a challenge to the class such as:

- Fastest to find... (a 'WOW' word, Power Opener or similar)
- Fastest to identify a Power Feature in the child's own writing or that of a partner or the imaginary friend.

This can be more fun when played 'against the clock'.

22 Spot the Subject

This is done by looking at sentences and asking children to stop and describe each or all of the following:

- What is the sentence about?
- Who is the subject?
- Where is the sentence set?
- What do you think is about to happen?
- Where is the event taking place?

23 Imaginary Friend forgets... game

- Put up a passage from 'Marmaduke' with all punctuation, including capital letters missing.
- The class read the passage out loud, naming the missing punctuation as they come to the place where it is needed, and drawing the missing piece large in the air with their finger. Include the capital letters in the process.

NB. This game can also be played identifying 'Marmaduke's' errors in spelling and grammar.

24 Alliteration Games

Teachers can play a range of games such as:

- Identifying alliterative words that would apply to a given thing/noun, e.g. a puppy, flower, bicycle or a mouse.
- Creating sentences that have strings of alliterative words. For example: *The substantial stegosaurus swaggered into the sumptuous swamp.*

In addition to all of the above, teachers might use some of the electronic *Big Writing Games* or *VCOP Games* available on CD ROM from www.andrelleducation.co.uk.

How do I choose a stimulus for the Big Write writing session?

The stimulus for writing is usually chosen from aspects of learning that:

- Are linked to the wider curriculum
- Are provoked through the wider curriculum
- Will make children, especially boys, want to write.

Teachers should 'think outside the box' in order to plan interesting and provocative situations that give genuine, or apparently genuine, reasons to write. The following are just two examples of how this might be done:

Whilst studying Henry VIII in history, the teacher reports that the King has accused the Head Teacher of a serious crime and is holding him/her prisoner in the Tower of London. The class could then:

- Hold a general debate (linked to Citizenship) on the rights and wrongs of imprisonment. The writing could be linked to this, either as discursive (discussion text) or as a journalistic report.
- Debate whether they should intervene to rescue the Head Teacher, or allow the justice system to run its course. Steer this debate towards the need to write a persuasive letter to the King, protesting the Head Teacher's innocence and pleading for his/her release.
- Recall the features of a letter through studying five letters that have been sent to the teacher's house recently.
- Review and remind themselves of the features of persuasive writing using the poster or similar that was used to teach that text type.

- Complete a Talk Homework using the following instruction slip: 'My homework tonight is to talk with you about things we could say to Henry VIII that would persuade him to release the Head Teacher, and please can we turn the TV off for this?'

Whilst studying Natural Disasters in geography, the teacher could rush in and announce that there is a tornado warning for their area. The class could then:

- Read reports on tornadoes, including how they form, and their potential size and force.

- Role play being in a huge storm.

- Watch the opening part of *The Wizard of Oz*.

- Write explanations for how tornadoes form for an encyclopaedia or web site.

- Study newspaper and magazine reports on the impact of massive tornadoes.

- Discuss what impact a tornado would have on the locality of the school.

- Write newspaper reports about the locality being hit by a tornado.

- Research 'What to do if there is a tornado warning'.

- Study instructions for safety drills and write similar instructions for 'How to Survive a Tornado'.

- Complete a Talk Homework using the following instruction slip: 'My homework tonight is to talk with you about things we would need to include in instructions for ways to survive a tornado, and please can we turn the TV off for this?'

Equally, the stimulus for writing can be in response to stories, myths, legends, fables or poems being studied in English, or linked to a current event or aspect of popular culture such as a new film, TV show or computer game with which all children are familiar.

How do I choose the text type?

The text type for the Big Write should always be one that has already been taught, so that children can focus on extending their VCOP skills and improving their Basic Skills, rather than worrying about the features of a 'new' type of writing.

The ideal teaching sequence for teaching text types should be planned by Senior Leaders in the school and each class teacher given a 'map' that shows within which theme/s each text type is taught and reinforced across Key Stage 2. This process is explained in more detail in *Raising Writing Standards: A powerful and effective whole-school approach* by Ros Wilson, (OUP, 2012).

If there is ever a situation where this has not been done, a teacher would need to consider which themes he or she is planning to teach across the year and allocate the teaching of text types to the themes where they seem to have the greatest relevance. This allocation should then be given to Senior Leaders and the English subject leader for approval.

Teachers should strive for balance, with between three and five weeks allocated to each unit, depending on:

- The degree of challenge in understanding the features of the text. For example, instructions are relatively simple and formulaic, and should be familiar to children, whereas a discursive text is more challenging and may not be introduced until Year 5 in some schools.

- Whether the class has had previous teaching of the text type and so already has partial understanding.

Teachers should be prepared to be flexible, observing children's learning closely to determine whether they have allocated too little or too much time to allow thorough understanding, and be prepared to adjust the time allocation accordingly or plan a quick return to the same text type in another theme.

How do I prepare the class for the Big Write?

During the week leading up to the Big Write session teachers should be doing the daily Basic Skills work, as well as 'Stocking Fillers' and 'Bells Work' (*see page 27*) to secure the VCOP skills needed (and, for subsequent sessions, those skills identified during observations as needing further reinforcement).

The day before the Big Write the teacher should:

1 Inform children of the text type to be written the next day and briefly review its main features (*see page 14 for exemplification*).

2 Establish the scenario for the stimulus or purpose for the writing (*see page 13 for exemplification*).

3 Give every child a Talk Homework slip to take home (*see page 14 for exemplification*).

How and why do I change the environment for the Big Write?

The weekly Big Write session is divided exactly in half by morning playtime, with the second half of the session being devoted to silent extended writing. During the morning playtime the teacher, with help from two pupils, should prepare the classroom for the silent writing by dimming the lighting and playing classical music, preferably Mozart, at a very low volume (*see page 14*).

The environmental changes may sound a bit extreme to some teachers but they are specifically designed to give a clear message to the children that:

- This session is different from a usual lesson.

- This session is special – and so is the work we do in it.

- This session is held in silence.

- This session is about concentration and absorption in the writing process.

- You need to forget your friends and what is around you.

- You are free to 'lose' yourself in the writing experience.

- It's time to ENJOY being a writer.

If you expect silence and create the right atmosphere, you may be surprised at how positively children respond.

What are the 'Time Prompts' during the Big Write?

The 'Time Prompts' during the Big Write serve the practical purpose of reminding children how long they have had, how long they still have, and what they might need to review within their writing to ensure it is of the best standard. They also serve the added purpose of providing quick 'brain breaks' for children, whose concentration may flag after about 8-10 minutes.

During the silent writing session the teacher should:

- Sit and model concentration and the pleasure of silent writing. This is a good opportunity to complete the Imaginary Friend's writing.

- Give the time prompts, pointing up at the clock at the appropriate points:

  1 "You have been writing for 10 minutes, how many sorts of punctuation have you used?"

  2 "You have been writing for 20 minutes, how many 'WOW' words have you used?"

  3 "You have been writing for 30 minutes, how many Power Openers have you used?

  4 "You have 5 minutes left. You need to complete your writing."

The time prompts work best when the clock has had colour coding added to divide it into 10 minute sections. This can be done by using a highlighter to 'colour' the alternate 10 minutes.

The sequence of the time prompts is important. We would not normally want children to use three or more 'WOW' words or Power Openers within the first 10 minutes of writing, but three different sorts of punctuation would contribute to a lively or powerful opening. Children must be taught to count 'sorts of' punctuation rather than 'pieces of'. Children must also be taught how to finish off work within a five-minute warning. By the end of the second term of Year 6, children should be able to use the clock independently to pace themselves.

How do I mark the weekly Big Write work?

It should take at least five minutes to mark each child's writing thoroughly. The teacher would not normally use the Oxford Writing Criterion Scale to mark every piece of work, but should have a sound understanding of the Standard at which each child is working, and should respond to any piece of writing that is substantially below (or indeed above) their expectations.

- Underline (neatly and discretely) at least three strengths in the writing. These will normally be Power Features (WOW words, Power Openers or Power Punctuation).

- Give specific feedback on the strengths by noting in the margin, for example, 'Great WOW word'.

- Underline (neatly and discretely) up to three areas for improvement. These may be Basic Skills or areas for up-levelling. Try and ensure there are always more strengths identified than areas for improvement.

- Give specific feedback on the areas for improvement by noting in the margin, for example, 'Sp = their' or 'Use an adjective'.

- Write a short paragraph at the bottom of the writing that:

  - comments on the response to the stimulus

  - comments on the use of features of the text type

  - comments on the use of VCOP

  - gives up to three areas for improvement.

The following is an example of such a paragraph:

"Well done Ryan, this is a really good effort. I enjoyed your explanation; it was interesting, clear and thoughtful with all the right features. You used a good range of 'WOW' words and it is good to see you starting to use a wider range of punctuation. Please try to use one or two Power Openers next week and keep working on the handwriting."

What are 'Stocking Fillers'?

Stocking Fillers are short, 5 minute sessions, designed to revisit aspects of VCOP taught the previous week and identified in observation and marking as needing further reinforcement. They can be used in lessons across the curriculum.

There should be 4 or 5 'Stocking Fillers' a week. These are usually achieved by tightening up on the time allowed for completing the activity part of foundation subjects, such as history, geography and religious education. Too often, children 'wander' their way through activities at a fairly leisurely pace. Teachers should tell children precisely how long they have to complete the activity and count down with 5 minute time prompts to 'push' the children into working at a brisker pace. In this way time will be freed for insertion of 'Stocking Fillers' within or between lessons.

- Each 'Stocking Filler' should last about 5 minutes.

- Each 'Stocking Filler' is a repeat of one of the activities or games from the last oral session.

- One element only, of the activity or game, should be changed for interest or for extension.

- Each 'Stocking Filler' might be a different activity or game, or one particular one might be repeated three times in a changed form, if the teacher feels the children need more practice.

For example, if the teacher has introduced the purple balls (*see page 21*) for the first time in a Big Write Oral Session, the next week she might re-use the original purple ball activity in one 'Stocking Filler' session:

In the Big Write Oral Session, put a Purple Ball on each table in the class.

- Ask children to make up games that use the ball.

- Ask children to throw the ball to a random group member.

- When a child catches the ball, they make up a sentence that includes... (the WOW word or Power Opener closest to the child's pointing finger or thumb).

In a 'Stocking Filler' he or she might then:

- Give out the purple balls with new 'WOW' words on and repeat the same game.

- Give out the purple balls with the same 'WOW' words and play a different game.

- Give out the purple balls with the same OR different 'WOW' words on, and tell the children they must make up a sentence that includes TWO WOW words (the WOW words or Power Openers closest to both the child's pointing fingers or thumbs).

What is 'Bells Work'?

'Bells Work' is the repeated, frequent oral use of new words and sentence structures in the spare few minutes that occur, even in the busiest classrooms, throughout the week. These small re-enforcements of learning to embed new language are usually found when the class has finished their work, tidied their tables and is waiting for the bell to go for assembly, playtime, lunchtime or to go home, or while waiting for shared space such as the hall for Physical Education or the library or ICT Suite. Like Stocking Fillers, they can be used where relevant in lessons across the curriculum.

The teacher usually asks the class to, "Make me up a sentence that has _____ in," or "Make me up a sentence that starts with _____". Often the teacher gives a context for the sentences and this can link well with learning across the whole curriculum. For example, "Make me up a sentence with the word 'inspirational' in, about Damian's painting yesterday."

What are the 3 pieces of fruit or sweets for?

Motivation through small rewards is a key part of *Big Writing* because we are often dealing with children who are disaffected with the writing process. Of course, in an ideal world, making progress and 'doing well' should be reward enough for most children, but the reality is that for some pupils, instant gratification can encourage them to 'have a go' even if just to win the reward. As the pupils begin to make and recognise their own progress – and feel proud of their achievements – the need for rewards diminishes.

During the oral part of the Big Write session, teachers might use small chocolates or sweets to reward pupils for good responses and suggestions. During the silent writing part of the session, grapes or other fruit are provided as rewards for children as they achieve their personal goals.

Teachers of children who are moving from Standard 2 (Year 1) to a secure Standard 3 (Year 2) will find they need to teach the children how to increase the length of a piece through the '5 Ws' (What, When, Where, Who, Why) and through detail and description. Setting up to three personal goals for children, related to these features and to VCOP, is a useful way of helping them to focus their efforts.

At each Time Prompt (*see page 25*) children are encouraged to review what they've written and think about these personal goals. When they feel they've achieved each goal, they may eat a piece of fruit.

What do the end of year Standards look like?

In the primary phase of education, most children progress from a very basic level of mark-making through to a confident, fluent standard, where basic skills are mostly accurate and they are able to make informed choices about writing structure and style.

Standard 1 (end of YR/P1)

Uses emerging phonics knowledge to write words that are spelt to reflect the way they speak and can spell some common, single syllable words correctly. They can make up their own simple sentences and can write at least 3 that an adult can read without the help of the child or others. (May be technically inaccurate.)

Standard 2 (end of Y1/P2)

Writing is a good paragraph in length; the writer is aware of full stops and capital letters but does not always use them correctly. Simple conjunctions such as 'and', 'but' or 'so' are used and all but the more complex words are accurately spelled and readable.

Standard 3 (end of Y2/P3)

Developing: Writing is close to 100 words in length and around 50% accurate in use of full stops and capital letters. Neat, accurate handwriting with most single syllable words spelled correctly and most other words decodable. Writing uses a range of openers and 2 or more different connectives.

Secure: As above but close to a side of A4 and around 80% accurate in use of full stops and capital letters, with neat, joined handwriting. Spelling is mostly accurate with just a few words that can't be read.

Child is beginning to use connectives such as 'if', 'when' and 'because' as well as some adjectives.

Advanced: As above but at least a side of A4 with a wider range of punctuation and connectives and both adjectives and adverbs used. Verb tenses are used correctly and the writer is beginning to use a range of strategies to create 'flow'.

Standard 4 (end of Y3/P4)

A side of A4 and mostly accurate but often boring or dull; alternatively, writing is creative and lively but weak in basic skills/accuracy.

Standard 5 (end of Y4/P5)

A side of A4 or more, creative, and around 80% accurate in basic skills and use of specific text type features.

Standards 6 and 7 (end of Y5/P6 or Y6/7)

A side and a half or more of writing that is 90% accurate is all aspects. For Standard 7 this rises to 99% accuracy with well-controlled use of a range of sophisticated language and features.

The **four generic targets: VCOP** are common to all Standards of writing from Standard 3 (Year 2) upwards, and from Standard 6 (Year 5) they are the elements that increase the sophistication of the writing. It is the person's repertoire and confidence in applying these four elements in increasingly challenging contexts that raises the standard of the writing.

The explicit teaching, development and practice of these skills is at the heart of the *Big Writing* approach to moving children up through the age-related expectations.

Progression in teaching and learning

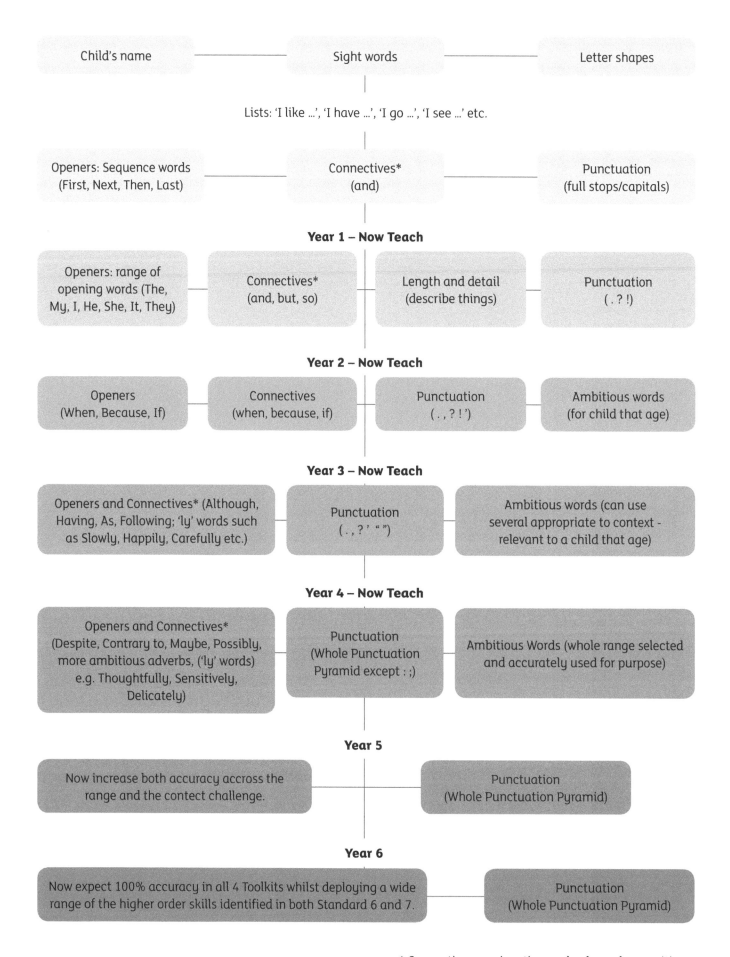

Child's name —————— Sight words —————— Letter shapes

Lists: 'I like …', 'I have …', 'I go …', 'I see …' etc.

| Openers: Sequence words (First, Next, Then, Last) | Connectives* (and) | Punctuation (full stops/capitals) |

Year 1 – Now Teach

| Openers: range of opening words (The, My, I, He, She, It, They) | Connectives* (and, but, so) | Length and detail (describe things) | Punctuation (. ? !) |

Year 2 – Now Teach

| Openers (When, Because, If) | Connectives (when, because, if) | Punctuation (. , ? ! ') | Ambitious words (for child that age) |

Year 3 – Now Teach

| Openers and Connectives* (Although, Having, As, Following; 'ly' words such as Slowly, Happily, Carefully etc.) | Punctuation (. , ? ' " ") | Ambitious words (can use several appropriate to context - relevant to a child that age) |

Year 4 – Now Teach

| Openers and Connectives* (Despite, Contrary to, Maybe, Possibly, more ambitious adverbs, ('ly' words) e.g. Thoughtfully, Sensitively, Delicately) | Punctuation (Whole Punctuation Pyramid except : ;) | Ambitious Words (whole range selected and accurately used for purpose) |

Year 5

| Now increase both accuracy accross the range and the contect challenge. | Punctuation (Whole Punctuation Pyramid) |

Year 6

| Now expect 100% accuracy in all 4 Toolkits whilst deploying a wide range of the higher order skills identified in both Standard 6 and 7. | Punctuation (Whole Punctuation Pyramid) |

* Connective = conjunctions, adverbs and prepositions.

Exemplar of progression

The following examples take a single piece of writing and demonstrate progression in style and skills from E.Y.F.S./YR to Year 6.

All examples, except E.Y.F.S./YR are too short to achieve their standard as they are presented here. They should be considered excerpts only. The errors in the examples are intentional and would be acceptable at the standards assessed.

E.Y.F.S./YR

The dog is big. The dog likes a bone. the dog can bark. I like the doge.

Year 1

The dog is big. The dog likes a bone. the dog can bark. And the dog can run. I like the dog and I like the cat.

Year 2 Developing

My dog is big and brown and very scrufy. He like to eat bones but he like sausages best. My dog can bark loudly and he can run very fast. I like my cat and my dog but I like my dog best.

Year 2 Secure

Have you seen my dog? He is big and brown and very scruffy. He likes to eat bones, and sausages and biskits too but he likes sausages best. My dog can bark very loudly and he can also run very fast. I like both my dog and my cat but I like my dog best.

Year 3 Developing

I have two pets, a dog, and a cat. I like them both, but I like my dog best. He is large, brown, and very scruffy. My dog likes eating bones, sausages, and biscits but he likes eating sausages best. I cover my ears when my dog barks because it is loud. He also runs very fast.

Year 3 Secure

I have two pets, a dog, and a cat. I like them both but I like my dog best! He is large, rusty brown and very scruffy. Have you seen him? He looks very funny. My dog likes eating bones and biscuits, but best of all he likes eating saosages. When my dog barks it is so loud that I cover my ears. Also my dog runs very fast.

Year 4 Developing

Although I have two pets I like my dog best. You should see him! He is large, rusty brown and very scruffy. He does look very funny. My dog enjoys eating bones and biscuits however he enjoys sausages most of all. When my dog barks it is so loud, I just have to cover my ears. Have you heard him?

Year 4 Secure

People often ask me about my pets. Although I have two pets, I like my dog best. You should see him! He is large, rusty brown and very scruffy. He looks so very funny, have you seen him? His diet is mainly bones and biscuits, which he enjoys, however he enjoys sausages most of all. When my dog barks it is so loud! I just have to cover my ears for protection.

Year 5 Developing

People often ask me about my pets and although I have two, I have to say I like my dog best. That large, rusty brown ragamuffin looks so very amusing that he makes me laugh. Have you seen him? He mainly dines on biscuits and bones, however he prefers meat and he enjoys sausages most of all. When my scruffy, old friend barks it is as loud as Concord, crashing through the sound barrier. We all have to cover our ears for protection.

Year 5 Secure

People often ask me about my pets and although I have two, I have to say that if I have to choose my favourite is my dog. Can you picture a large, rusty brown ragamuffin with a comical face who looks at you with such an amused expression that you have to laugh? That's my Bonzo! His diet is fairly simple, he mainly dines on biscuits and bones. If given a choice, however, he prefers meat, and most of all he enjoys a juicy beef sausage. Although Bonzo is a very dear and loving friend he has one fault. When he barks it is as if Concorde is breaking the sound barrier! The whole family has to cover their ears for fear of damage.

Year 6 Developing

'Man's best friend is his dog.' It's an old saying, but a very true one. Although I have two pets, a dog and a cat, I have to say that, if forced to choose, the former is my favourite. Picture, if you will, a large, russet-brown ragamuffin with a comical face, whose amusing expression regards you with such pathetic appeal that you are obliged to laugh. That's my Bonzo! When he is hungry, his expression becomes even more pathetic, so that even the sternest of masters would submit to his pleading gaze. His dietary requirements are fairly simple, he mainly dines on biscuits and bones. For preference, however, he would dine on meat and most of all he enjoys a succulent beef sausage. Bonzo is a very dear and loving friend, however he does have one quite serious fault. When he barks it is as if a thousand Concordes are shattering the sound barrier! Our entire family cover their ears, afraid that his tortured cries might cause lasting damage.

Year 6 Secure

"Man's best friend is his dog." It's an old saying, but a very true one! Although I have two pets, a dog and a cat, I have to say that – if forced to choose – the former is my favourite. Picture, if you will, a sturdy, russet-brown ragamuffin with a comical facial expression that is both quizzical and amusing as he regards you with such pathetic appeal that you are obliged to laugh. That's my Bonzo! When hungry, his facial features portray an even greater pathos, rendering even the sternest of masters defenceless to his pleading. Certainly, he knows how to wind humans round his finger! Dietary requirements for my faithful friend are surprisingly simple, he dines predominantly on biscuits and bones; his preference, however, would be a diet of fresh, lean meat and he salivates in ecstasy at a whiff of a succulent sausage. Despite being a dear and affectionate friend, Bonzo does, however, have one (but only one) quite serious fault. Whenever he barks, it is as though a thousand Concords are shattering the sound barrier! Our entire family hastily cover their ears lest his tortured cries render their hearing forever damaged.

How do I secure children's basic skills?

There are four basic skills that impact on achievement in writing. They are:

- Accurate **grammatical structure**
- **Handwriting**
- **Spelling**
- Basic sentence structure and **punctuation**.

They can be given the acronym **GHaSP** as a useful hook for children if needed.

Large numbers of children are held back as writers through a lack of confidence and/or expertise in two or more of the four basic skills. More importantly, poor basic skills can 'drag down' a child's level during assessment.

Grammatical structures and Talking Posh!

Accurate grammatical structures for writing are best developed through oral activities. Children need to learn a special formal 'voice' for writing, known in *Big Writing* as 'Talking posh'. 'Talking posh' is a fun way to help children develop the correct 'writing voice' in their heads and build their VCOP skills. It provides a model for the higher order language structures to be used in good writing.

It is important to explain to children that this voice is purely for writing, and that their normal 'speaking voice' – with all its character, community significance and heritage – is still highly valued.

- Tell children that in order to write well we need to have a 'posh' writing voice inside our heads.
- Use fun role-play scenarios to introduce posh talk – e.g. a visit from the queen or a duchess or similar.

> **"If a child can't say it, a child can't write it!"**

- Introduce one 'posh' lesson a week, in which you teach through posh talk – i.e. using a humorous, overtly formal voice to orally demonstrate the higher order language structures found only in writing, for example: 'Having keenly awaited the conclusion of play time we are now fully prepared to commence our pre-lunch activities.'
- Build discussion in to the activities that requires pupils to use posh talk.
- Nominate pupils to be the 'talk police' and shout out if they spot grammatical errors.
- Naturally, the teacher makes frequent errors and pupils greatly enjoy the fun of shouting at and correcting him/her!

You can move this lively 'posh' lesson through different subjects each week to keep it fun and fresh.

Handwriting

Schools should expect all children to develop neat, joined writing by the time they leave Key Stage 1. If we expect 100% we will get much closer to that than if we say not all pupils can get there.

The particular style taught in a school is not the most important aspect, as long as it achieves a neat, flowing and legible hand. The most important factor is the consistency with which all adults teach, model and promote the school style, using it in every aspect of their work in the school. Teachers saying that all pupils must do something one way, then doing it a different way themselves, can lead some children, particularly boys, to regard this as unfair! Children have a great sense of fairness and may become disaffected if something is seen as unfair.

Every child should be taught handwriting pro-actively as long as is necessary for him/her to develop a neat, flowing, joined style. They should then be given interesting activities to consolidate their style.

At the beginning of each term (or half term if handwriting is a particular issue), all pupils should be taken back to basic letter formation and first joining patterns, addressing the full process again within two weeks to arrive back at the level at which they are currently working. A talented TA who is a good modeller of the school style could also run intervention clinics – perhaps 10 minutes a day – at the beginning of each year for high priority children in Key Stage 2.

Spelling

Word lists for the years previous to the year a child is working in should be recycled intensively at the beginning of each year, or re-taught through weekly 10 minute sessions if needed. It's also important to do a quick review of phonics – basic letter sounds, digraphs and blending – and irregular high frequency words.

Recycling learning in this way must be LIVELY and FUN! Disaffected learners who are falling behind will not be motivated by rote learning and dull, repetitive exercises. It's vitally important to design interesting, active and enjoyable ways for pupils to access or revisit learning they have missed.

The new year's list of words should be taught in a separate session, alongside new phonic skills as needed. *High Frequency Word Games* are available on disc from www.andrelleducation.co.uk and include games for the word lists for all years and also WOW words.

Basic sentence structure and punctuation

There is evidence that many young children do not 'hear' the writing voice clearly inside their heads, and that they will be more successful if they are actively encouraged to speak their writing out loud as they work.

If a child is struggling with basic sentence structure (as shown by the use of a full stop and capital letter), a skilled writing partner or a TA or teacher should consistently read back every piece of the child's writing with him/her, in order to help him/her to identify the ends of sentences and insert full stops and capital letters.

The Punctuation Pyramid

The Punctuation Pyramid, shown in full on page 65, illustrates progression in punctuation and is a useful tool for *Big Writing*. Pupils at all stages should be encouraged to know and name each type of punctuation, even if they are not yet ready to use them correctly in their own writing. Teachers should:

- Refer to the pyramid every time pupils write in any subject.

- Play games by covering items with post-its and asking pupils to name what is missing.

- Play fun, lively oral games by using – and misusing – punctuation in sentences so that children can understand the effect of the punctuation on the meaning or expression of a sentence.

Recycling basic skills

Too many teachers in Key Stage 2 dismiss the teaching of basic skills as the job of Foundation and Key Stage 1, and do not understand the importance of offering children a fresh chance to learn these skills.

Teachers wrongly assume that pupils get bored by recycling because we, as adults, do. It is not the recycling that bores children but dull, unimaginative teaching. The key is to make basic skills work fun, lively and as varied as possible, using a wide range of opportunities across the school day.

In *Big Writing* we recommend five 10-minute Basic Skills sessions each week, as shown opposite. These sessions should be lively and fun, and should recycle basic skills throughout Key Stage 2, returning briefly at the start of each term to the very first steps in each skill and moving quickly forward. In addition, the basic skill of accurate grammatical structures should be addressed through talk.

How do I do the formal assessments?

Three times a year – usually in September, December and May – teachers should assess

their pupils' work formally using The Oxford Writing Criterion Scale (*see Appendix 1*) on an extended piece of writing that has been produced with no teacher input or support, other than ensuring the children understand the task. Children should be given 10 minutes 'thinking' time and 45 minutes to write.

There should be:

- No time prompts in Key Stage 2 other than the '5 minutes to finish' warning.

- No visible VCOP (or similar) displays.

- Nothing on the white board other than the title of the piece and, if necessary, the text type.

- The usual changes to the environment for writing.

DAY	BASIC SKILL
1	**Spelling – irregular high frequency words/sight words** ● Recycle word lists from previous years ● Use laminated cards to play 'snap' or matching games
2	**Spelling – phonics for encoding** ● Recycle phonic skills from previous years ● Move rapidly through early phonic skills such as single letter sounds, simple blends and digraphs ● Make up fun nonsense words ● Ask pupils to use a dictionary to find challenging words and ask other pupils to attempt the spellings
3	**Spelling – new irregular words or new phonic skills** ● Teach any new words or phonic skills for the year ● Use games, flash cards, air writing, writing in sand etc
4	**Handwriting** ● In early phases, before a fluent style is established, revisit letter formation, joining letters etc as needed ● Once a fluent style is established, pupils can practise presentation skills by, for example, recording a piece of their work or making an anthology of poems, jokes etc
5	**Times tables (if not known)** ● Teach them proactively and in a lively, engaging way ● Revisit times tables daily to embed this key maths skill

- Each child might have a drink on the table, either water or juice.

Full guidance on how to assess writing using the Oxford Writing Criterion Scale is provided in Appendix 1.

What do I do if I am a teacher in the Early Years Foundation Stage (EYFS)?

The role of practitioners in the EYFS in preparing children for *Big Writing* is the development of oral language skills through 'Talk the Big Talk'.

'Talk the Big Talk' is the extension of language through:

1 A team planned focus for teaching each week. This might be a new connective, a 'WOW' word, a varied sentence structure, use of an adjective or adverb (describing words) or similar.

   - Create opportunities to introduce and use the feature in all areas of learning, which are planned by the team and used by all.

   - Maximise spontaneous opportunities to repeat and consolidate use at every opportunity.

   - Celebrate across the team whenever a child is heard using the feature in their play.

2 Planned opportunities for discussion and debate in response to exciting stimuli such as:

   - The discovery of something unusual or interesting within the unit, for example: an artefact down the back of the armchair, a strange 'creature' under the rug or in the role play corner, a mysterious object appearing on a table or chair or in the home corner or similar.

   - An unexpected and mysterious event in the environment, such as: strange, oversize footprints in the wilderness area, evidence that a spaceship may have landed on the outdoor play area, a strange object that can be seen on the edge of the roof, or similar.

   - The unexpected arrival of an interesting character (including in fancy dress costume) in the unit, such as: Alice in Wonderland, Mickey Mouse, a pirate, the Queen, or similar.

   - The arrival of an important member of the community in the unit, such as: a community nurse or police officer, a local celebrity, a famous sporting figure or similar.

   - An adult in the unit arriving wearing: a strange wig or hat, a strange mask or the face of a known character or person, a fancy dress costume.

   - The arrival at the unit of a live animal such as: someone's pet, a farm animal, a horse or pony, a creepy crawlie.

3 Maximising the curricular opportunities for high quality discussion and use of language in response to learning in contexts such as:

   - Drama and role play
   - Poetry
   - Story
   - Film and multimedia
   - Dance
   - Artefacts
   - Art and music
   - Scientific investigations and experiments
   - Gardening and growing seeds
   - Games and physical activity
   - Field trips
   - Field study
   - New experiences over a wide range of the curriculum.

For more detailed guidance on the importance of talk in the EYFS and beyond see *Talk the Big Talk*, by Ros Wilson, (OUP, 2012).

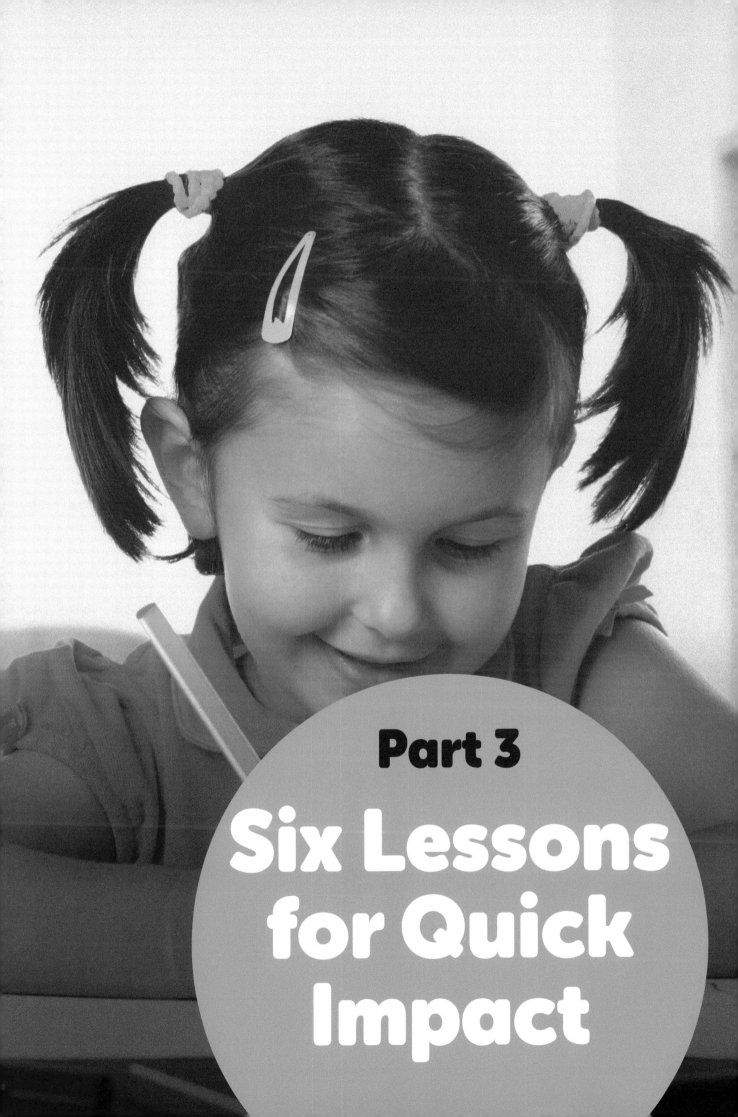

Part 3

Six Lessons
for Quick
Impact

03: Six Lessons for Quick Impact

These lessons are designed for upper Key Stage 2 children*. They are planned to be taught in two sessions of between 45 and 55 minutes each, ideally straddling a playtime within the same morning. Additional time - 10 to 15 minutes - should also be allocated to allow children to proof read, edit and improve their work. This will require an adjustment of the timetable to allow a whole morning to focus on raising writing standards.

The lessons do not need to be taught over consecutive weeks. In fact, for children with significant progress to make, they are best taught at two or three week intervals with opportunities for consolidation built in to the interim weeks. All the short activities and taught inputs can be re-planned and taught with small changes to keep things fresh. Timings are approximate and the pace of the lesson will be affected by pupils' responses.

The same lesson plans and Lesson Support Materials, adapted for children in Year 2 and/or Year 3, are provided in Appendix 5.

A different text type should be written by the children in each of the interim weeks.

After the first lesson, pupils should be given a Writing Portfolio in which to keep their handouts and work.

The most important thing is to keep these lessons lively, pacey and fun.

The Lesson Support Materials (LSM) referenced in each lesson plan are provided in Appendix 4. Three additional LSMs for extension, plus a 'Skill Kit' reference sheet, are also provided.

All lesson plans, ideas and support materials are intended to be adapted and adjusted to suit the needs of your particular pupils.

LESSON ONE: Part one

Key objective: to recognise and use VCOP

Objective	Activity	Differentiation	Resources
1 Can we show what we know about punctuation and connectives?	**Warm up (15 mins)** Ask children to recall/name a range of punctuation and scribe on the whiteboard. Ask volunteers to come up and illustrate examples named by using in a sentence. Now ask children to name a range of connectives (or 'joining words') – you could give 'and' as an example and illustrate by using it to join two simple sentences. Give children pairs of sentences and ask them to say the connective they would use to join them. You could experiment with changing the connectives and discussing any change of meaning to the final sentence. If children do not know any connectives, plan taught input on them during English work.	Through group and/or adult support and by outcome. Some pupils may have had prior input to prepare them, so they are able to make a contribution or may have TA support.	LSM 1: Sentence pairs
2 Can we identify features that show higher levels in writing?	**Taught (15 mins)** Give children two texts – one at a very low level and one, the same text, but at a higher level. Ask children to read both texts quietly in pairs and then play 'Spot the Difference'. Discuss what makes the second text a higher level. Identify the range of connectives and punctuation used.		LSM 2: Up-levelling texts The Punctuation Pyramid (*see page 65*)
	Look at the sentence openers and vocabulary to emphasise that there are four ways to make writing a higher level. Introduce the punctuation pyramid. What do pupils think this represents? Identify the levels and explain the pyramid. Name together every piece of punctuation and review use of those known.		
3 Can we use what we have found?	**Short activity (15 minutes)** Write a 'Standard 3' sentence on the board and challenge children, in pairs, to re-write the sentence at a higher Standard. (You may need to model this first.) This is more fun if done on scrap paper or mini-whiteboards. Come together and discuss interesting examples of the four features: VCOP. Select and model some of the ideas and compose a final new higher level sentence. Name this process: Up-Levelling.		Paper, pens or mini-whiteboards

LESSON ONE: Part two

Key objective: to recognise and use VCOP

Objective	Activity	Differentiation	Resources
	A brief review of what was said before BREAK about the four key features of writing: VCOP		
1 Can we show what we know about punctuation and connectives?	**Activity (25 mins)** Read 'The Monster' text together. In pairs, pupils identify elements of VCOP using highlighters or by underlining. Name a colour for each aspect of VCOP and model a couple of examples first if needed. Share likes and dislikes about the passage and talk about suspense. Record interesting/ambitious words.	Through peer support and by outcome. Pair less able with more able pupils or pair less able pupils with a TA for additional support.	LSM 3: The Monster Highlighter pens or coloured pens/crayons (four colours)
2 Can we identify features that show higher levels in writing?	**Writing activity (20 mins)** Pupils work individually to write next paragraphs to continue the story of 'The Monster'. Stop after 10 minutes and ask who has used more than one type of punctuation, an interesting sentence opener, more than two different connectives, and an interesting or unusual word. Offer praise and continue for a further 10 minutes, or more if children are productively engaged with the task.	By outcome. Pupils unable to write productively without support should be given scaffolds, model words/phrases and/or adult support as needed.	LSM 3: The Monster Lined paper and writing pens
3 Can we use what we have found?	**Plenary (10 minutes)** Collect work and explain that you will assess it and return. Discuss what the term 'assess' means. Review learning on the VCOP features of writing, against the lesson objective. Show pupils LSM 4 and explain how it works. Relate it to the VCOP features and explain that they will be looking at this in the next lesson.		LSM 4: My Target Record

LESSON TWO: Part one

Key objective: to recognise and use descriptive language

Objective	Activity	Differentiation	Resources
1 Can we show what we know from the last lesson?	**Warm up (15 mins)** What can pupils remember about the four features: VCOP? Collect examples from them and scribe, clustering under the headings Vocabulary, Connectives, Openers, Punctuation. Give children the mnemonic Very Clever Old Person (their teacher) to help them recall VCOP. Distribute the 'My Target Record' sheet and pupils' writing from the previous lesson. Pupils discuss the assessment and how the targets you have set link in to the Target Record sheet. Publish and discuss the objective of this lesson: descriptive language. Refresh content and use of the Punctuation Pyramid. Activity: Give oral quick-fire sentences for pupils to write or say the punctuation they would use.	Through group/adult support and by outcome. Some pupils may have had prior input to prepare them, so they are able to make a contribution or may have TA support.	LSM 4: My Target Record Assessed writing from the previous lesson The Punctuation Pyramid (*see page 65*)
2 Can we identify descriptive words?	**Taught (15 mins)** Display the text 'Howl'. Read and respond to the text. Identify VCOP features and collect. Link to assessment through the Target Record sheet Brainstorm more descriptive words for monsters – use language such as 'adjective' and 'adverb' as appropriate. Praise and reward children who score 'goals' relating to their targets.	Through peer support and by outcome. Some pupils may have had prior input to prepare them, so they are able to make a contribution or may have TA support.	LSM 5: Howl LSM 4: My Target Record
	Short activity (15 mins) Distribute the 'Monsters in Stories' handout. Pupils read softly in pairs and then choose ONE paragraph to focus on. Use highlighter pens to underline descriptive words and record them on a scrap piece of paper. Collect all examples and write up on the board.	Insert an easier paragraph to support less able pupils. For extension: do more than one paragraph or challenge pupils to extend the chosen paragraph by one or more sentences.	LSM 6: Monsters in Stories Highlighter pens or coloured pens/crayons (four colours)
	BREAK – followed by a brief review of what has been said about the four key features of writing: VCOP		

LESSON TWO: Part two

Key objective: to recognise and use descriptive language

Objective	Activity	Differentiation	Resources
3 Can we identify the VCOP?	**Short activity (15 mins)** Ask pupils to practise reading their chosen paragraph, with expression. Ask for volunteers to read to the class. Discuss the features of the text that help to inform expression. Use highlighters to identify the VCOP features. Play 'Find the Word' (max 5 mins). Give a word that is a synonym for a word in one of the paragraphs and ask pupils to find the word. Praise and reward pupils who score 'goals'.	Through peer support and by outcome. Pair less able with more able pupils or pair less able pupils with a TA for additional support.	LSM 6: Monsters in Stories
4 Can we respond to a descriptive text?	**Taught (5 mins)** Hand out copies of the text 'Howl'. In pairs, pupils read and respond to the text. Then read together as a class. Share likes/dislikes about the passage and talk about suspense. Tell pupils that they are going to continue writing the story. Review collections of words/phrases from the earlier session.	Through peer support and by outcome. Pair less able with more able pupils or pair less able pupils with a TA for additional support.	LSM 5: Howl
	Writing activity (20 mins) Pupils work individually to write the next paragraph to continue the 'Howl' story. Stop after 10 minutes and ask who has used more than one type of punctuation, an interesting sentence opener, more than two different connectives, and an interesting or unusual word. Offer praise and continue for a further 10 minutes, or more if children are productively engaged with the task.	By outcome. Pupils unable to write productively without support should be given scaffolds, model words/phrases and/or adult support as needed.	LSM 5: Howl
5 Can we say what we have learnt?	**Plenary (10 mins)** Ask the 'Who has used …?' questions again and invite suggestions. Praise and reward pupils. Collect work and explain that you will assess it and return. Discuss what the term 'assess' means. Review learning against the objective: descriptive language.	For less able, use closed questions, e.g. read a sentence then ask: 'Was that a question?' or 'Was the monster big?'	

LESSON THREE: Part one

Key objective: to find and use features of good writing

Objective	Activity	Differentiation	Resources
1 Can we show what we know about VCOP?	**Warm up (15 mins)** Do some quick-fire VCOP work: • Who can start a sentence with ...? • Who can make me up a sentence with ...? • Who can change the connective in this sentence to a higher level ...? • Who can name the punctuation at the end of this sentence? Use the LSM sheets and lists of ambitious vocabulary to support this session. Refresh content and use of the Punctuation Pyramid. Share the example of a pupil's work (don't reveal whose work it is). Read together and identify the VCOP features and any particularly good examples. Discuss likes and dislikes. Reveal the writer and offer praise – make them 'goal scorer of the week'. Publish and discuss the objective of this lesson: features of good writing. Activity: Give oral quick-fire sentences for pupils to write or say the different opener they would use.	Through group/ adult support and by outcome. Some pupils may have had prior input to prepare them, so they are able to make a contribution or may have TA support.	The Punctuation Pyramid (*see page 65*) LSM 7: Openers LSM 8: Connectives A list of ambitious vocabulary already collected A (good) example of a child's work from previous lesson (with minimal edits so that it makes sense)
2 Can we identify the VCOP?	**Taught (15 mins)** Display the letter from a friend to an expelled pupil. Read the letter together. Discuss its layout and identify good features, focusing on VCOP and descriptive language.		LSM 9: Expelled!
3 Can we use what we know?	**Short activity (15 mins)** Write a simple sentence on the board and ask pupils to work in pairs to 'up-level' it using VCOP features. Pupils can then work together to write a 'P.S' sentence for the letter. Share good examples. Praise and reward children with 'goals'.	Through peer support and by outcome. Pair less able with more able pupils or pair less able pupils with a TA for additional support.	LSM 9: Expelled!
	BREAK – followed by a brief review of what has been said about the four key features of writing: VCOP		

LESSON THREE: Part two

Key objective: to find and use features of good writing

Objective	Activity	Differentiation	Resources
4 **Can we identify features that show higher levels in writing?**	**Activity (25 mins)** Give pupils copies of LSM 9. Ask them, in pairs, to read through it and identify elements of VCOP using highlighters or underlining. Share findings and likes and dislikes about the letter. Discuss what might really have happened.	Through peer support and by outcome. Pair less able with more able pupils or pair less able pupils with a TA for additional support.	LSM 9: Expelled! Highlighter pens or coloured pens/crayons (four colours)
5 **Can we use what we have found?**	**Writing activity (20 mins)** Pupils work individually to write a reply to the letter. Stop after 10 minutes and ask who has used more than one type of punctuation, an interesting sentence opener, more than two different connectives, and an interesting or unusual word. Offer praise and continue for a further 10 minutes, or more if children are productively engaged with the task.	By outcome. Pupils unable to write productively without support should be given scaffolds, model words/phrases and/or adult support as needed.	LSM 9: Expelled! Lined paper and writing pens
6 **Can we say what we have learnt?**	**Plenary (10 mins)** In pairs, pupils use the 'My Target Record' to estimate the Standard of each other's writing. Ask the 'Who has used …?' questions again and invite suggestions. Praise and reward pupils. Collect work and explain that you will assess it and return. Discuss what the term 'assess' means. Discuss two short excerpts from pupils' writing that you identified whilst they were writing. Ask the class to say why you chose these pieces as good examples. Discuss VCOP features. Review learning against the objective: features of good writing.	For less able, use closed questions.	LSM 4: My Target Record

LESSON FOUR: Part one

Key objective: to recognise and use features of good writing

Objective	Activity	Differentiation	Resources
1 Can we show what we know about VCOP?	**Warm up (15 mins)** Do some quick-fire VCOP work as per Lesson Three. Share the examples of pupils' work. Read them together and ask why these excerpts have been chosen. Ask pupils to identify the VCOP features. Return pupils' work and compare with their targets. Offer praise and reward. Publish and discuss the objective of this lesson: features of good writing.	Through group/ adult support and by outcome. Some pupils may have had prior input to prepare them, so they are able to make a contribution or may have TA support.	A collection of good examples of sentences or short passages from children's work from previous lesson (with minimal edits so that they make sense) Make sure that over time you include examples from every child, editing as necessary. LSM 4: My Target Record
2 Can we use features that show higher standards in writing?	**Short activity (10 mins)** Give the letter to pupils and ask them, in pairs, to 'be the teacher' and edit it to correct the errors. As an extension, pupils could 'up-level' the writing by inserting new VCOP features	Through peer support and by outcome. Pair less able with more able pupils or pair less able pupils with a TA for additional support.	LSM 10: Be the teacher
3 Do we know the structure of a story?	**Taught (15 mins)** Distribute the Story Structure Cards. Ask pupils with the sequence words to come out and stand where they think they should be in the story OR use the washing line and pegs. Then ask pupils with the content words – What, When, Where etc – to come and stand in the part of the story they think they might be. Ask questions such as: 'What sort of Who/What/ Where might you get in the story opening?' Finally, ask pupils with the 'feelings' words to come out and attach these to the content words. Ask them to explain what sort of feelings there might be in that part of the story.	Less able take the Sequence words More able take the content words ('W' words) Higher ability take the 'feelings' words	LSM 11: Story Structure Cards Washing line and pegs (optional)
4 Can we plan a story?	**Planning (10 mins)** Give a title for the unsupported writing. Make a single bubble map or list ideas. Discuss as a class then make a planning map. (*See Appendix 3*)		Scrap paper, pencils/pens or mini-whiteboard

LESSON FOUR: Part two

Key objective: to recognise and use features of good writing

Objective	Activity	Differentiation	Resources
	BREAK – followed by a brief review of four key features of writing: VCOP and planning maps.		
5 **Can we identify features that show higher standards in writing?**	**Writing activity (45 mins)** Remind pupils of the title for the unsupported writing. Remind them of the visual stimulus if used. Remind pupils of their targets and of the story structure work done in the earlier session. Pupils work individually to write their story. They stop after 15 and 30 minutes and pass their work to a partner. They ask each other the 'Who has used …?' questions and offer praise. The writing partners might also do a quick check for VCOP features. Pupils continue writing for a further 15 or 20 minutes, with a five minute warning given before the end.	By outcome. Pupils unable to write productively without support should be given scaffolds, model words/phrases and/ or adult support as needed.	Lined paper and writing pens
6 **Can we recognise good features in our partner's work?**	**Plenary (10 mins)** Pupils exchange writing with their writing partner. They read and identify examples of VCOP to share with the class. Review learning against the objective: features of good writing. Have we achieved it? Praise and reward pupils, then collect work for assessment.	Pair less able and provide TA support.	

LESSON FIVE: Part one

Key objective: to recognise and use features of good writing

Objective	Activity	Differentiation	Resources
1 Can we show what we know about VCOP?	**Warm up (5 mins)** Do some quick-fire VCOP work as per Lesson Three. Share the examples of pupils' work. Read them together and ask why these excerpts have been chosen. Ask pupils to identify which feature peers have used. Return pupils' work and compare with their targets from the previous lesson. Are they the same or have they changed? Offer praise and reward. Publish and discuss the objective of this lesson: features of good writing. What does this mean?	Through group/ adult support and by outcome. Some pupils may have had prior input to prepare them, so they are able to make a contribution or may have TA support.	A collection of good examples of sentences or short passages from children's work from previous lesson (with minimal edits so that they make sense) Make sure that over time you include examples from every child, editing as necessary. LSM 4: My Target Record
2 Can we find features of good writing?	**Short activity (15 mins)** Give the poem Mist and Moonlight (or a similar poem at the right level) to pupils and ask them, in pairs, to identify good/interesting features. Discuss, as a class, these features and how the writer uses descriptive language to create atmosphere.	Through peer support and by outcome. Pair less able with more able pupils or pair less able pupils with a TA for additional support.	LSM 12: Mist and Moonlight
3 Do we know the structure of a story?	**Taught (15 mins)** Review the structure of a story using the Story Structure Cards as a quick refresher. Discuss 'scary' things and collective descriptive words for scary things. Talk about how atmosphere is created in scary stories or movies – i.e. using the setting, lighting, weather, night time and so on. Make up a simple class scary story using the Story Structure Cards.	Less able take the Sequence words More able take the content words ('W' words) Higher ability take the 'feelings' words	LSM 11: Story Structure Cards
4 Can we plan a story?	**Planning (10 mins)** Give a title for the scary story. Use a visual stimulus if available. Record immediate ideas in a single bubble or list. Discuss as a class then make a planning map. (*See Appendix 3*)		Scrap paper, pencils/pens or mini-whiteboard

LESSON FIVE: Part two

Key objective: to recognise and use features of good writing

Objective	Activity	Differentiation	Resources
	BREAK – followed by a brief review of four key features of writing: VCOP and planning maps.		
5 Can we use the VCOP in unsupported writing?	**Writing activity (45 mins)** Remind pupils of the title for the unsupported writing. Remind them of the visual stimulus if used. Remind pupils of their targets and of the story structure work done in the earlier session. Pupils work individually to write their story. They stop after 15 and 30 minutes and pass their work to a partner. They ask each other the 'Who has used …?' questions and offer praise. The writing partners might also do a quick check for VCOP features. Pupils continue writing for a further 15 or 20 minutes, with a five minute warning given before the end.	Pupils unable to write productively without support should be given scaffolds, model words/phrases and/ or adult support as needed.	Lined paper and writing pens
6 Can we recognise good features in our partner's work?	**Plenary (10 mins)** Pupils exchange writing with their writing partner. They read and identify examples of VCOP to share with the class. Review learning against the objective: features of good writing. Have we achieved it? Praise and reward pupils, then collect work for assessment.	Pair less able and provide TA support.	

LESSON SIX: Part one

Key objective: to recognise and use features of good writing

Objective	Activity	Differentiation	Resources
1 Can we show what we know about VCOP?	**Warm up (15 mins)** Do some quick-fire VCOP work: • Play the Punctuation Pyramid Game • Write two simple sentences on the board for pupils to up-level Share the examples of pupils' work. Read them together and ask why these excerpts have been chosen. Ask pupils to identify which feature peers have used. Return pupils' work and compare with their targets from the previous lesson. Are they the same or have they changed? Offer praise and reward. Publish and discuss the objective of this lesson: features of good writing.	Through group/ adult support and by outcome. Some pupils may have had prior input to prepare them, so they are able to make a contribution or may have TA support.	A collection of good examples of sentences or short passages from children's work from previous lesson (with minimal edits so that they make sense) Make sure that over time you include examples from every child, editing as necessary. LSM 4: My Target Record
2 Do we know the structure of a story?	**Taught (15 mins)** Review the structure of a story. Give children a subject for writing. Record immediate ideas using a single bubble or by making a list. Discuss the ideas then make up a simple outline of the story, using the Story Structure Cards for support if needed.		LSM 11: Story Structure Cards (optional)
3 Can we recognise paragraphs?	Use a piece of text from a story or information text to review paragraphing.		A book or enlarged extract from a book to demonstrate paragraphs
4 Can we use a mind map to plan?	**Planning (10 mins)** Give a subject for the writing. This could be linked to the wider curriculum. Pupils work with a talk partner to make a mind map or other plan (*See Appendix 3*). Clearly identify the structure of the writing using the map or highlighter to identify sections.	Through peer support and by outcome. Pair less able with more able pupils or pair less able pupils with a TA for additional support.	Scrap paper, pencils/pens or mini-whiteboard

LESSON SIX: Part two

Key objective: to recognise and use features of good writing

Objective	Activity	Differentiation	Resources
	BREAK – followed by a brief review of four key features of writing: VCOP and planning maps.		
5 Can we use the VCOP in unsupported writing?	**Writing activity (45 mins)** Remind pupils of the title for the unsupported writing. Remind pupils of their targets and of the key elements of story structure. Remind pupils about paragraphs. Pupils work individually to write their story. They stop after 15 minutes and pass their work to a partner. They ask each other the 'Who has used …?' questions and offer praise. The writing partners might also do a quick check for VCOP features. Pupils continue writing for a further 15 or 20 minutes, then pass their work to their partner again. This time, the question is: 'Who has used paragraphs to structure their writing?' Continue for a further 15-20 minutes, with a five minute warning given before the end.	By outcome. Pupils unable to write productively without support should be given scaffolds, model words/phrases and/ or adult support as needed.	Lined paper and writing pens
6 Can we recognise good features in our partner's work?	**Plenary (10 mins)** Pupils exchange writing with their writing partner. They read and identify examples of VCOP to share with the class. Review learning against the objective: features of good writing. Have we achieved it? Praise and reward pupils, then collect work for assessment.	Pair less able and provide TA support.	

Part 4

Case Study

04: Case Study: Scorton CE Primary School

" ... highly charged and industrious learning environment. "

Could this really be our school? Following the impact of *Big Writing*, OFSTED thought so! Looking back over our adoption of *Big Writing* this has been the single most effective change in my teaching over 20 years. It's never too late to learn something new!

Background

Scorton CE Primary School is a very small, rural primary school set in the centre of an old Lancashire village. It serves the mixed local community which has a range of private and rented accommodation. A higher than average proportion of pupils join and leave the school other than at the usual points of admission and transfer. Pupils are taught in two mixed-age classes. One contains children in the Reception Year and pupils in Years 1 and 2; the other class contains pupils in Years 3, 4, 5 and 6.

In 2006, faced with a group of uninspired Year 6 boys and the end of year SATS lurking in the not so distant future I was surfing the internet when I came across *Big Writing*. Thinking it looked different from the usual diet of revision I decided to try the 'Strategies for quick impact' contained in the book *Strategies for Immediate Impact on Writing Standards* with my small group of Year 6 children. I enjoyed teaching the lessons and the children seemed to respond. SATs came and went and the 'project' came to an end.

Over the summer break I decided that the messages of *Big Writing* worked for me as a teacher and so swotted up and taught myself the basics, reading up and buying books. KS2 and Optional SATs results confirmed that standards in writing were considerably lower than reading. In September I began teaching *Big Writing* every week to my mixed class of Year 3, 4, 5 and 6 pupils and badgered my head teacher about it until she eventually sent me on the 'official' course. *Big Writing* really snowballed from there on.

I decided to ask the children what they liked about *Big Writing* and was both pleased and shocked by the results. Comments such as "It's fun!", "I know how to use more wow words", and "I like the grapes" were common but two comments really shocked me: "It gives us time to work quietly on our own" and "We get to think of our own ideas." I realised that in my mixed age class with our daily literacy lesson the children really didn't get many opportunities to write for themselves without me interrupting and asking them to follow a rigorous structure.

Gradually, I realised that the principles of *Big Writing* were present in every literacy lesson I taught; we were jiggling sentences every day, adding WOW words to the wall, using our writing voices, spotting power openers and brainstorming connectives, even up-levelling writing across the curriculum.

Following on from this we held INSET for our cluster of small schools, encouraging them to give it a go and sharing the pupils' comments, which most colleagues could also recognise within their own classrooms. In 2010 we decided as a school to extend *Big Writing* down to Key stage 1 and now every Thursday morning you'll find our whole school doing the 'Big Write'.

We purchased the *Big Writing* software games, spent time creating good quality resources and now track our writing using the B*ig Writing Criterion Scale Assessment Tool*. Assessment is done termly because staff feel confident in making accurate judgements, targets are set after each piece of writing that can be achieved the next week, as well as a half term target for the class that addresses key issues based on the four areas of V.C.O.P.

Each year we hold an open *Big Writing* lesson which parents can take part in – I don't know who worries most about this – staff, children or parents.

In May 2011 we had an OFSTED inspection. We chose to ask the Inspector to watch our Big Write in action and the report came back with the comments shown:

Year on year our writing results have improved and this year (2010-2011) everyone achieved Level 4 and 86% achieved Level 5 in writing. This year we have a very different cohort, our small numbers make target setting difficult but we are still aiming for 50% Level 5s in writing.

Thank you Ros and the team because these comments came about as a direct result of the *Big Writing* pedagogy and training. I can only encourage other teachers to give it a go, embrace the ideas, go on the training courses.

Helen Hesketh
April 2012
Scorton CE Primary School
Scorton
Preston
PR3 1AP

> ❝ ...learning moves on at an incredibly fast pace, the teacher's high expectations and pupils' thirst to learn creating a highly charged and industrious learning environment. In an English lesson, the teacher's expert subject knowledge and lively input at the start motivated pupils and prepared them very well for the writing task ahead. All worked diligently, with pupils explaining that the background music, 'Helps us to be creative'. Pupils produced writing of an exceptionally high standard for their ages. They used a wide range of descriptive vocabulary very effectively to create an atmosphere of suspense, spelt complex words correctly and used punctuation knowledgeably. ❞
>
> **OFSTED**

Part 5

Appendices

The Oxford Writing Criterion Scale

How to use the Oxford Writing Criterion Scale

The Oxford Writing Criterion Scale (OWCS) is designed to enable accurate, objective assessment of writing in schools and to be used to identify the next steps in a child's writing for them to make progress.

The OWCS is organized into a series of Standards that map to the primary year groups, from Standard 1 (Reception/P1) through to Standard 7 (Year/ P7). Each Standard sets out a number of criteria against which children are assessed.

It is recommended that a summative assessment is conducted once a term, e.g. in December, March and May/June, although some schools prefer a single 'end of year' assessment only. It is vitally important that summative assessments are carried out on a piece of writing that is truly independent and unsupported and which, from Standard 2 onwards, is close to a side of A4 or more in length.

The summative assessment process is as follows:

Step	What to do	Notes
Step 1	Set an appropriate independent writing task for assessment purposes. You may want to offer children a choice of stimulus but it is important to ensure that every child is writing to the same text type.	*The OWCS can be used to assess all text types, although poetry, recount of a known story and narrative are not, usually, useful genres for assessment.*
Step 2	Select the appropriate OWCS Standard for the year group of the child, or children, you wish to assess.	*If you know, from other assessments or knowledge of a child, that a child is working well below expectations select the Standard from the prior year.*
Step 3	Photocopy a Standard for each child – adding their name and the date of the assessment.	
Step 4	Read through the piece of writing carefully. Then complete the OWCS using the following marks to indicate your judgement against each criterion: ✔ –there is clear, secure evidence in this piece that the child has mastered this skill ● –there is some evidence in this piece that the child is beginning to do this ✗ – there is no evidence in this piece that the child can do this (this could also indicate skills that have not been taught yet)	*You should expect to see three good examples to make a secure judgement although two particularly strong examples may be sufficient. At the higher Standards, one accurate and effective example of e.g. metaphor or the subjunctive would be acceptable.* *Remember: even if you think a child is secure or developing in a skill from previous work you must base your summative judgement on the evidence in this piece only.*
Step 5	Sometimes the text type or genre of the piece means that one or more criteria cannot be assessed. Each criterion that cannot be assessed should be marked with a dash [-].	
Step 6	Add up the number of ticks to generate a score and use the box at the bottom of the Standard to make a judgement.	*If one or more criteria are marked with a dash, reduce the points required to achieve each category accordingly. For example, if 'Developing' requires a score between 6–9 points it can be awarded for a score between 5–8 points if one criterion is unassessed or between 4–7 points if two criteria are unassessed.*
Step 7	If the piece of writing does not make the entry threshold for 'Developing' at the required Standard for the year group you should assess against the Standard for the prior year. If the piece of writing reaches an Assessment Point for a particular Standard you may assess against the Standard for the next year. However, if the piece does not meet the entry threshold for 'Developing' at the next Standard it should be recorded as 'Advanced' at the current Standard.	*This child will need focused support and intervention to help them make accelerated progress.* *You will want to ensure that this child has opportunities to broaden and deepen their skills within the Standard for their year group, as well as providing stretch in the form of new learning, as appropriate.*
Step 8	Children's basic skills – spelling, handwriting, punctuation – any 'pre-requisite' criteria listed on the Standard and those criteria marked with a dot ⊠ can be used to inform the child's immediate next steps.	
Step 9	Retain the assessed piece of writing and the OWCS judgement in a class folder of evidence. Use a spreadsheet to record the pattern of assessments across the class over an academic year.	

PRE-WRITING STANDARD: Early Years		
Name:	Date:	

No	Criteria	Evidence? (✔, ✗, ●)
1	Will tolerate hand manipulation.	
2	Will work with another to allow mark-making using body parts or an implement.	
3	Will attempt to mark-make independently.	
4	Can recognize mark-making materials.	
5	Can use and enjoys mark-making materials.	
6	Can show some control in mark-making.	
7	Can produce some recognizable letters.	
8	Can differentiate between different letters and symbols.	
9	Shows some awareness of the sequencing of letters.	
10	Can copy over/under a model.	
11	Can imitate adults' writing and understands the purpose of writing.	
12	Can name three or more different purposes of writing.	
13	Can ascribe meaning to own mark-making ('reads' what has been 'written').	
14	Knows print has meaning and that, in English, it is read from left to right and top to bottom.	
15	Can write the initial letter of their own name.	
16	Can attempt to 'write' things, including their own name, using random letters.	
17	Can write their own name, although it may be with wrong letter formations or mixed lower/upper case.	
18	Can recognize their own first name when it is written in clear print.	

Standard 1: Reception/P1		
Name:	Date:	

No	Criteria (listed in an approximate hierarchy)	Evidence? (✔, ✗, ●)
1	Can draw recognizable letters of the alphabet.	
2	Can write their own name.	
3	Can 'write' things using a mix of appropriate and random letters.	
4	Can sequence most of the letters of the alphabet.	
5	Can write their own name with the correct letter formations, although the size and shape may be slightly inconsistent.	
6	Can name the purpose of different texts/types of writing (at least three).	
7	Can 'read' what he/she has 'written'.	
8	Can hold and use a pencil effectively.	
9	Can spell some of the words from the Year R High Frequency Word list.	
10	Can spell CVC (consonant, vowel, consonant) words (e.g. sit, bag, cat) usually correctly.	
11	Can write simple labels and captions.	
12	Can usually leave a space between emerging words.	
13	Can show some control over word order, producing short logical statements, trying to use emergent phonics for spellings not known.	
14	Can produce two or more logical statements on the same subject.	
15	Can spell many words on the Year R High Frequency Word list.	
16	Is beginning to attempt to write simple known stories.	
17	Can say what they want to write, speaking in clearly defined statements or sentences.	
18	Can spell many common, single syllable words correctly in writing, including most of the words in the Year R High Frequency Word list and the Early Years Outcomes.	
19	Can write three or more simple statements on a given subject that can be read without the child's help and that make sense, although letter shapes and spelling may not be fully accurate.	

Assessment score	
0–2 ticks = not yet working at this Standard; review against Pre-Writing Standard.. 3–8 ticks = Developing 9–16 ticks = Secure	17–19 ticks = Advanced Assessment point: children with 18 or more ticks may be assessed against Standard 2

STANDARD 2: Year 1/P2	
Name:	Date:

No	Criteria	Evidence? (✔, ✗, ●)
1	Can write their own first name with appropriate upper and lower case letters (may not be totally accurate).	
2	Can form all letters clearly, although size and shape may be irregular.	
3	Writes simple regular words, some spelt correctly.	
4	Almost always leaves spaces between words.	
5	Makes sensible phonic attempts at words.	
6	Can spell all CVC (consonant, vowel, consonant) words (e.g. sit, bag, cat) correctly.	
7	Confidently writes some captions and labels and attempts other simple forms of writing (e.g. lists, stories, retellings etc.).	
8	Can show some control over letter size, shape and orientation in writing.	
9	Can say what their writing says and means.	
10	Can retell known stories in writing.	
11	Can produce their own ideas for writing (not a retelling).	
12	Can show some control over word order, producing logical statements.	
13	Can spell most of the Year R and 1 High Frequency Words and the Year 1 words in the National Curriculum. Appendix 1.	
14	Can make recognizable attempts at spelling words not known (almost all decodable without the child's help). (If all are spelt correctly, tick this criterion so as not to penalize the child).	
15	Can write simple texts such as lists, stories, reports, recounts (of a paragraph or more).	
16	Begins to show awareness of how full stops are used in writing. (May be in the wrong places or only one, final full stop.)	
17	Can usually give letters a clear and regular size, shape and orientation (ascenders and descenders and use of upper and lower case are usually accurate).	
18	Can use ANY connective (may only ever be 'and') to join two simple sentences, thoughts, ideas, etc.	
19	Can use appropriate vocabulary (should be coherent and sensible) in more than three statements.	
20	Can always use logical phonic strategies when trying to spell unknown words in more than three statements.	
21	Can usually use a capital letter and full stop, question mark or exclamation mark to punctuate sentences.	
22	Can produce a paragraph or more of developed ideas independently that can be read without help from the child (may be more like spoken than written language but must not be a retelling).	

Assessment score	
0–6 ticks = not yet working at this Standard; review against Standard 1. 7–12 ticks = Developing 13–17 ticks = Secure	18–22 ticks = Advanced Assessment point: children with 20 or more ticks may be assessed against Standard 3.

STANDARD 3: Year 2/P3		
Name:	Date:	

No	Criteria	Evidence? (✔, ✗, ●)
1	Can communicate ideas and meaning confidently in a series of sentences of at least a paragraph in length. (May not be accurate, but mainly 'flows' as it has lost the 'list like' form typical of some early writing.)	
2	Can control use of ascenders/descenders and upper/lower case letters in handwriting.	
3	Can write in three or more text forms with reasonable accuracy. (If the writing is a narrative, simple report or recount of a known story, this cannot be ticked as they should already know these three text forms. If it is another genre, it can be ticked).	
4	Can provide enough detail to interest the reader (e.g. is beginning to provide additional information or description beyond a simple list).	
5	Can vary the structure of sentences to interest the reader (e.g. questions, direct speech or opening with a subordinate clause, etc.).	
6	Can sometimes use interesting and ambitious words (they should be words not usually used by a child of that age, and not a technical word used in a taught context only, e.g. 'volcano' in geography or 'evaporate' in science).	
7	Can usually sustain narrative and non-narrative forms (can write at length – close to a side of A4 at least – staying on task).	
8	Can match organization to purpose (e.g. showing awareness of the structure of a letter, openings and endings, the importance of the reader, organizational devices, beginnings of paragraphing, etc.).	
9	Can usually maintain the use of basic sentence punctuation (full stops followed by capital letters) in a piece close to a side of A4 in length. (May be on a shorter piece or may not be accurate to achieve the 'Developing' category.)	
10	Can spell most common words correctly and most of the Years R, 1 & 2 High Frequency Words, and the Year 1 & 2 words in the National Curriculumn. Appendix 1.	
11	Can use phonetically plausible strategies to spell or attempt to spell unknown polysyllabic words. (If all the spelling is correct in a long enough piece to provide secure evidence, tick this criterion.)	
12	Can use connectives other than 'and' to join two or more simple sentences, thoughts, ideas, etc. (e.g. but, so, then, or, when, if, that, because).	
13	Can use a range of punctuation, mainly correctly, including at least three of the following: full stop and capital letter, exclamation mark, question mark, comma (at least in lists), apostrophe for simple contraction and for singular possession (at least), e.g. 'John's dog...', 'The cat's bowl...'.	
14	Can make their writing lively and interesting (e.g. provides additional detail, consciously uses humour, varies sentence length or uses punctuation to create effect, etc.).	
15	Can link ideas and events, using strategies to create 'flow' (e.g. Last time, also, after, then, soon, at last, and another thing...).	
16	Can use adjectives and descriptive phrases for detail and emphasis (consciously selects the adjective for purpose, rather than using a familiar one, e.g. a title: 'Big Billy Goat Gruff').	
17	Structures basic sentences correctly, including capitals and full stops in a longer piece (one error is acceptable).	
18	Can use accurate and consistent handwriting (in print at a minimum, can show consistent use of upper/lower case, ascenders/descenders, size and form).	
19	Begins to show evidence of joined handwriting.	
20	Uses past and present tenses correctly.	
21	Can produce close to a side (or more) of A4 writing that is clear and coherent with one or more strong features.	

Assessment score	
0–5 ticks = not yet working at this Standard; wreview against Standard 6–9 ticks = Developing 10–16 ticks = Secure	17–21 ticks = Advanced Assessment point: children with 18 or more ticks may be assessed against Standard 4.

STANDARD 4: Year 3/P4

Name: Date:

No	Criteria	Evidence? (✔, ✗, ●)
1	Can produce work which is organized, imaginative and clear (e.g. simple opening and ending).	
2	Can usually join their handwriting.	
3	Can use a range of chosen forms appropriately and consistently. (If the writing is a narrative, simple report or recount of a known story, this cannot be ticked as they should already know these three text forms. If it is another genre, it can be ticked).	
4	Can adapt their chosen form to the audience (e.g. provide information about characters or setting, make a series of points, use brackets for asides, etc.).	
5	Can sometimes use interesting and ambitious words (they should be words not usually used by a child of that age, and not a technical word used in a taught context only, e.g. 'volcano' in geography or 'evaporate' in science).	
6	Can develop and extend ideas logically in sequenced sentences (but they may still be overly detailed or brief).	
7	Can extend sentences using a wider range of connectives to clarify relationships between points and ideas (e.g. when, because, if, after, while, also, as well).	
8	Can usually use correct grammatical structures in sentences (nouns and verbs generally agree).	
9	Can use pronouns appropriately to avoid the awkward repetition of nouns.	
10	Can use most punctuation accurately, including at least three of the following: full stop and capital letter, question mark, exclamation mark, comma, apostrophe.	
11	Can structure and organize work clearly (e.g. beginning, middle, end; letter structure; dialogue structure).	
12	Is beginning to use paragraphs.	
13	Can adapt form and style for purpose (e.g. there is a clear difference between formal and informal letters; use of abbreviated sentences in notes and diaries, etc.).	
14	Can write neatly, legibly and accurately, mainly in a joined style.	
15	Can use adjectives and adverbs for description.	
16	Can spell phonetically regular or familiar common polysyllabic words accurately (sometimes for the 'Developing' category) and most or all of the Year 3 High Frequency Words and the Year 3 words in the National Curriculum Appendix 1.	
17	Can develop characters and describe settings, feelings and/or emotions, etc.	
18	Can link and relate events, including past, present and future, sensibly (afterwards, before, also, after a while, eventually, etc)	
19	Can attempt to give opinion, interest or humour through detail.	
20	Can use generalizing words for style (e.g. sometimes, never, always, often, mainly, mostly, generally, etc.) and/or modal verbs/the conditional tense (e.g. might do it, may go, could rain, should win).	
21	Is beginning to develop a sense of pace (writing is lively and interesting).	

Assessment score	
0–5 ticks = not yet working at this Standard; review against Standard 3. 6–9 ticks = Developing 10–17 ticks = Secure	18–21 ticks = Advanced Assessment point: children with 19 or more ticks may be assessed against Standard 5.

STANDARD 5: Year 4/P5	
Name:	Date:

No	Criteria	Evidence? (✔, ✗, ●)
1	Can write in a lively and coherent style.	
2	Can use a range of styles and genres confidently and independently. (If the writing is a narrative, simple report or recount of a known story this cannot be ticked. If any other genre, it can be ticked as they will already know these three text forms.)	
3	Can sometimes use interesting and ambitious words (they should be words not usually used by a child of that age, and not a technical word used in a taught context only, e.g.' volcano' in geography or 'evaporate' in science).	
4	Can organize ideas appropriately for both purpose and reader (e.g. captions, headings, bullets, fonts, chapters, letter formats, paragraphs, logically sequenced events, contextual and background information etc.).	
5	Can use a wide range of punctuation mainly accurately, including at least three of the following: full stop and capital letter, question mark, exclamation mark, apostrophe and comma.	
6	Can write neatly, legibly and accurately, usually maintaining a joined style.	
7	Can use more sophisticated connectives (e.g. although, however, nevertheless, despite, contrary to, as well as, etc.).	
8	Can use links to show time and cause.	
9	Can open sentences in a wide range of ways for interest and impact.	
10	Can use paragraphs, although they may not always be accurate.	
11	Can produce thoughtful and considered writing (uses simple explanation, opinion, justification and deduction).	
12	Can use or attempt grammatically complex structures (e.g. expansion before and after the noun: 'The little, old man who lived on the hill...', '... by the lady who taught me the guitar...'; subordinate clauses: 'I felt better when...', etc.).	
13	Can spell unfamiliar regular polysyllabic words accurately and most or all of the Year 4 High Frequency Words and the Year 4 words in the National Curriculum. Appendix 1.	
14	Can use nouns, pronouns and tenses accurately and consistently throughout.	
15	Can use apostrophes and/or inverted commas, mainly accurately. (If direct speech is not appropriate to the task, apostrophes alone can score the tick).	
16	Can select from a range of known adventurous vocabulary for a purpose, with some words being particularly well chosen.	
17	Can select interesting strategies to move a piece of writing forward (e.g. asides, characterization, dialogue with the audience, dialogue, etc.).	
18	Can advise assertively, although not confrontationally, in factual writing (e.g. 'An important thing to think about before deciding...', 'We always need to think about...', etc.).	
19	Can develop ideas in creative and interesting ways.	

Assessment score	
0–5 ticks = not yet working at this Standard; review against Standard 4. 6–9 ticks = Developing 10–15 ticks = Secure	16–19 ticks = Advanced Assessment point: children with 17 or more ticks may be assessed against Standard 6.

No	Criteria	Evidence? (✔, ✗, ●)
	STANDARD 6: Year 5/P6	
	Name: Date:	
1	Can produce well-structured and organized writing using a range of conventions in layout.	
2	Can use appropriate informal and formal styles with confidence (e.g. conversational, colloquial, dialect, Standard English).	
3	Can select the correct genre for audience and purpose, and use it accurately.	
4	Can select from a wide range of known imaginative and ambitious vocabulary (they should be words that are not usually used by a child of that age) and use them precisely. (All spelling, including that of complex words, is almost always correct.)	
5	Can use paragraphs consistently and appropriately.	
6	Can group things appropriately before or after a main verb (e.g. 'The books, the pens and the pencils were all ready on the table').	
7	Can use all grammar accurately except when consciously using dialect or colloquialism for purpose and audience.	
8	Can use different techniques to open or conclude work appropriately (e.g. opinion, summary, justification, comment, suspense or prediction).	
9	Can use complex sentence structures appropriately.	
10	Can use a wider range of punctuation, almost always accurately, to include three or more of the following (as appropriate to the text): comma, apostrophe, bullets, inverted commas, hyphen, brackets, colon or semi-colon.	
11	Can use punctuation appropriately to create effect (e.g. exclamation mark, dash, question mark, ellipsis).	
12	Can write neatly, legibly and accurately in a flowing, joined style.	
13	Can adapt handwriting for a range of tasks and purposes, including for effect.	
14	Can spell accurately in all but the most complex words (e.g. paraphernalia, quintessential etc.) and most or all of the Year 5 High Frequency Words and the Year 5 words in the National Curriculum Appendix 1.	
15	Can use the passive voice for variety and to shift focus (e.g. 'The cake was eaten by the child').	
16	Can use a range of narrative techniques with confidence, interweaving elements when appropriate (e.g. action, dialogue, quotation, formal or informal style, aside, observation, suspense).	
17	Can vary sentence length and word order confidently to sustain interest (e.g. 'Having achieved your goals at such an early age, what motivates you to continue? Why fight on?').	
18	Can use a range of devices to adapt writing to the needs of the reader (e.g. headings, sub-headings, bullets, underlining, parenthesis, introduction providing context, footnote, contents, bibliography).	
19	Can use literary features to create effect (e.g. alliteration, onomatopoeia, figurative language, dialect, metaphor, simile etc.).	
20	Can interweave implicit and explicit links between sections.	
21	Can use punctuation to show division between clauses, to indicate, to vary pace, to create atmosphere or to sub-divide (e.g. commas, colons,semicolons, dashes, ellipses).	
22	Can show confident and established 'voice'.	

Assessment score

0–7 ticks = not yet working at this Standard; review against Standard 5. 8–11 ticks = Developing 12–18 ticks = Secure	19–22 ticks = Advanced Assessment point: children with 20 or may ticks may be assessed against Standard 7.

	STANDARD 7: Year 6/P7	
Name:	Date:	

No	Criteria	Evidence? (✔, ✗, ●)
1	Can spell all vocabulary correctly apart from rare technical or obscure words. (Must have used unusual, ambitious vocabulary that is spelt correctly.)	
2	Can open and close writing in interesting, unusual or dramatic ways, when appropriate.	
3	Can use the full range of punctuation accurately and precisely, including for sub-division, effect, listing, direct speech, parenthesis, etc.	
4	Can write neatly, legibly, accurately and fluently, in a joined style.	
5	Can vary font for effect or emphasis when appropriate (print, italics or capitalization). There may only be one example.	
6	Can use a wide range of conventions appropriately to the context, e.g. paragraphs, sub and side headings, addendum, footnote, contents, etc.	
7	Can use a wide range of sophisticated connectives, including conjunctions, adverbs and prepositions, to show time, cause, sequence and mode, including to open sentences sometimes.	
8	Can use clauses confidently and appropriately for audience and purpose.	
9	Can use implicit links within a text, e.g. referring back to a point made earlier or forward to more information or detail to come.	
10	Can use complex groupings for effect, before or after the verb. (For example: 'How I love the warmth of the summer breeze, the lapping of the waves and the soft swishing of the sand beneath my sandals.') There may only be one example.	
11	Can use a range of techniques to interact or show awareness of the audience, e.g. action, dialogue, quotation, aside, suspense, tension, comment.	
12	Can write with maturity, confidence and imagination.	
13	Can adapt writing for the full range of purposes, always showing awareness of audience and purpose.	
14	Can consciously vary levels of formality according to purpose and audience.	
15	Can sustain a convincing viewpoint throughout the piece of writing, e.g. authoritative, expert, convincing portrayal of character, opposing opinions, etc.	
16	Can use a wide range of ambitious vocabulary accurately and precisely (they should be words that are not usually used by a child of that age).	
17	Can use two or more stylistic features to create effect within the text, e.g. rhetorical questions, repetition, figurative language, passive voice, metaphor, simile, alliteration, onomatopoeia, groupings, elaboration, nominalization, impersonal voice, universal appeal (such as 'Everyone agrees that…').	
18	Can use creative and varied sentence structures when appropriate, intermingling with simple structures for effect.	
19	Can always construct grammatically correct sentences, unless using dialect or alternative constructions consciously for effect.	

Assessment score	
0–5 ticks = not yet working at this Standard; review against Standard 4. 6–9 ticks = Developing 10–15 ticks = Secure	16–19 ticks = Advanced Assessment point: children with 17 or more ticks may be assessed against Standard 6.

The Punctuation Pyramid

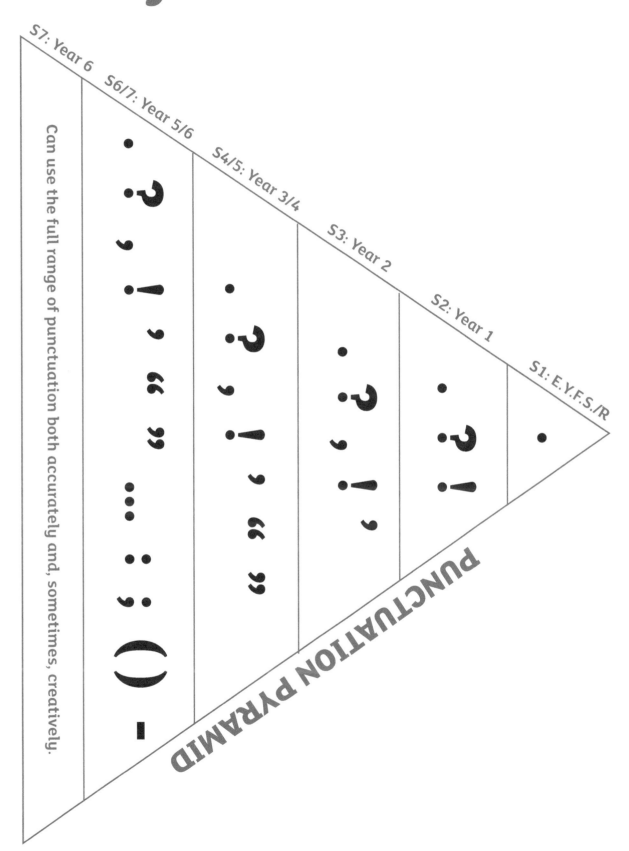

Planning for Writing

Planning for writing is a sensitive area. Different learning styles impact on pupils' attitudes to planning. Some pupils do not value planning at all, and find it tedious and pointless, which leads to demotivation before the writing process even starts. Other pupils benefit from time invested in planning, but may not equally value the methods offered.

It is useful to teach pupils – ideally in Year 1 – several different ways to plan a piece of writing, and then to allow them to choose the method that works best for them. As well as teaching them these different methods, and the general benefits of planning ahead, you should also give pupils the confidence to understand that the planning 'tools' you give them are there to help and should not be an onerous or enforced part of the writing process.

Keep the planning process short and quick whenever you model writing, but be flexible at the opening of writing time so that those who wish to can spend a little longer gathering and organising their thoughts.

Pupils may also show different attitudes to planning on different days. Allow them to show their individuality through their choice of planning method, and if a pupil does not wish to plan one week, encourage them to draw or annotate illustrations of key characters instead, or to collect ambitious words and phrases appropriate to the task.

The following are some of the ways of planning that work for many pupils.

1 The cartoon strip

1	2	3
4	**5**	**6**

This may have four, six or eight frames depending on age or the degree of support needed. Pupils may write or draw the sequence of events in a story, report, set of instructions etc.

2 The single bubble

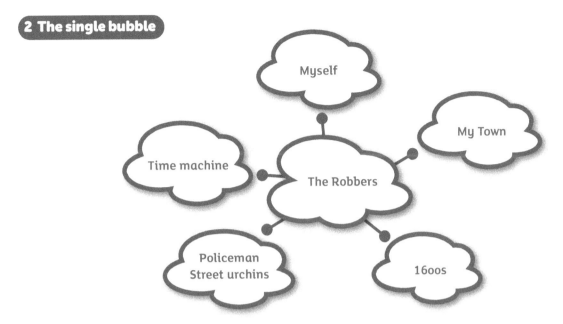

Pupils put the title or the main character, setting, event or idea in the middle bubble, then jot all their first thoughts down in the bubbles around it.

3 The mind map

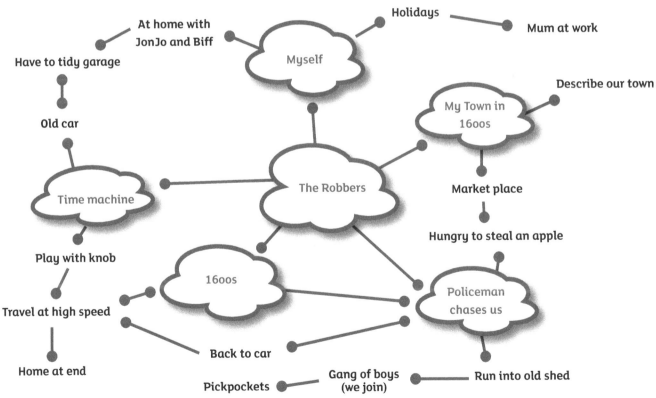

Pupils put the title or main idea in the middle, then follow their thoughts out in a web-like formation based on themes or sequenced events. Using different coloured pens or pencils to track each part of the web can also help.

4 The traditional scaffold

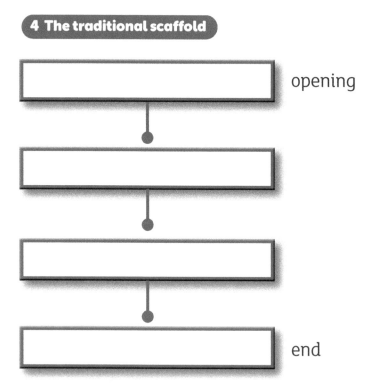

opening

end

Pupils use a series of boxes, like a flow chart, to support the linear organisation of ideas.

5 Clouds

Pupils use a series of 'thought clouds' to capture their ideas, and then connect them up using arrows if needed to make links between the ideas.

6 Lists

Pupils simply list their thoughts and ideas and jot notes down around the listed items, drawing arrows to link ideas, and making small sketches to visualise things if needed.

7 Planning partners

Oral discussion is a useful way of planning and 'thinking aloud'. Give pupils five minutes to talk (only) with a partner, then they can decide whether to switch to a recorded model or continue the discussion, or get on with the writing!

8 Story Structure Cards (see LSM 11, page 81)

Pupils can use the cards as a framework for planning, usually with a planning partner or an adult for support.

9 Talk Homework

Give every child a Talk Homework slip to take home to encourage discussion of ideas for what to write about.

Lesson Support Materials

These materials are designed for use within the six quick impact lessons set out in Part 3 of this book. They can also be used as quick warm-ups and 'stocking fillers' at other times of the week. Three additional LSMs, plus a 'Skill Kit' reference sheet, are also provided to support extension work.

The materials can be photocopied and used as hand-outs, or recreated on an interactive whiteboard.

All materials are provided as exemplars, and can be adapted and adjusted to suit the needs of your particular pupils.

LSM 1: SENTENCE PAIRS

I got up late.	I missed the bus.
I was hungry.	There was no food.
It was cold.	I put on my coat.
I like my cat.	I like my dog more.
BUT	AND
SO	BECAUSE
THEREFORE	HOWEVER

Big Writing: Six Lessons for Quick Impact © Andrell Education Ltd, 2012

LSM 2: UP-LEVELLING TEXTS

1 It was a dark night. Sally looked out of her window. She had been reading her book but thought she heard a noise. A man hurried past. He looked up and then crossed the street. Sally saw that he had a strange face. Then the man disappeared in to the park.

2 Sally peered from her window and out into the inky black night. She was certain that she had heard something. A cat screeched and some bins clattered, then all was silent again. Sally turned her attention back to the book she had been reading but she couldn't concentrate. Someone was coming, she was certain of it.

Just then, the stillness of the night was shattered by the sharp sound of footsteps on the pavement below. A hooded figure hurried past, clutching a small package. The figure turned and looked up the street before crossing the road. Horrified, Sally ducked down below the window sill to avoid being seen. The man, if it was a man, had the whitest face she had ever seen!

Raising her head back up again she looked out of the window to see the figure disappear in to the park. The darkness swallowed him. Sally shuddered.

Big Writing: Six Lessons for Quick Impact © Andrell Education Ltd, 2012

LSM 3: THE MONSTER

With fear and dread I crept cautiously down the dark, damp tunnel. My hands were my eyes, nervously seeking the way by tracing the slime-covered granite walls. Though I strained to hear and see, there was nothing ... nothing but the sounds of my own strained breathing and the soft pad of my rubber-soled shoes.

Suddenly an evil odour invaded my nostrils, like the rotting filth of a thousand corpses. I stopped, heart pounding. Was something there in the dreaded darkness? No longer able to stand not knowing, I pulled out my flashlight and switched on its harsh beam to light up the tunnel ahead.

Silence, heavy and still, surrounded me. Reassured, I began to step forward, when out of the black depths came a blood-curdling shriek as the great beast leapt towards me. There, pinned in the beam of my flashlight, I finally saw what it was ...

_____

_____

_____

_____

_____

_____

_____

_____

_____

Big Writing: Six Lessons for Quick Impact © Andrell Education Ltd, 2012

LSM 4: MY TARGET RECORD

Pupils keep these records in the front or back of their writing portfolio. They highlight those 'can do' statements that they have evidenced in unsupported writing. They star targets they are working towards.

Pupils use their Target Records as prompt sheets in the early stages of the *Big Writing* Quick Impact initiative, getting ideas for VCOP features from it to use in their writing. They may use it to help them to estimate the level they are writing at, or to 'up-level' a piece of text.

Punctuation	Connectives	Sentence openers
Level 1: I can use a few full stops, not always in the right place.	**Level 1:** I can join two sentences using any connective, e.g. **and.**	**Level 1:** I can use simple words to open sentences: **The ... My ... I ...**
Level 2: I can usually use full stops in the right place. I can always put a capital letter after a full stop. I can try to use question marks and commas.	**Level 2:** I can use three connectives: **and, but, so.** I can sometimes use **because, when.**	**Level 2:** I can open sentences with words that show the order things happened: **First, Next, Then, Last.** I can open sentences with simple connectives: **But ... So ... Then ...**
Level 3: I can always use full stops followed by a capital letter, in the right places. I can always use question marks in the right places. I can usually use commas and exclamation marks in the right places. I can try to use apostrophes in the right places to shorten words. I can try to use speech marks.	**Level 3:** I can use connectives to start sentences, e.g. **Before, After, If, As well as ...**	**Level 3:** I can open sentences with harder words to show the order (sequence) things happened: **Also ... After ... Soon ... Another thing ... Because ...**
Level 4: I can always use commas in the right places for both lists and pauses. I can always use speech marks in the right places. I can usually use apostrophes in the right places to shorten words and to show belonging. I can try to use other sorts of punctuation, e.g. **ellipses, dashes, colons, semi-colons.**	**Level 4:** I can use harder ways to start and to join sentences, e.g. **although, however, besides, even though.**	**Level 4:** I can use harder connectives to open sentences: **Although, Besides, Even though, Before.** I can use interesting ways of opening sentences: **After a while, Meanwhile, Before very long.**

Big Writing: Six Lessons for Quick Impact © Andrell Education Ltd, 2012

LSM 5: HOWL

Who would have thought such small creatures could have made so much noise? Valiantly I struggled on, clearing a path through the teeming throng of tiny people as they rushed frantically away from the entrance to the temple.

"Turn back," they cried. "Turn back, before it is too late!" But I had no choice. I had to press on into the gloomy stillness because the lives of too many people were depending on the success of my mission.

Strangely, inside seemed peaceful after the panic and confusion outside. I stood quietly, adjusting to the semi-darkness and listening carefully for any sound that would reveal the whereabouts of my foe. All was quiet ... too quiet! I waited.

After what seemed to be a very long time, but in reality might have been a few minutes, I crept forward, picking a careful path between the tumble of chairs scattered by the tiny people in their flight. Not a sound did I make, as I approached the doors to the crypt at the back of the temple. My hand was resting on the giant iron handle when through the vaulted ceiling echoed the demented scream of a tortured spirit, rippling and bursting from the shadowed depths of the bell tower. It was the haunted howl of death itself ...

Big Writing: Six Lessons for Quick Impact © Andrell Education Ltd, 2012

LSM 6: MONSTERS IN STORIES

1 After days and days of journeying they came to a wide tract of open country, in the midst of which they found a giant pillar of black stone like a furnace chimney, and sunk to his armpits in the pillar there was a creature the like of which none had seen before. He had two great wings and four limbs, two like human arms and two like lion's paws, with claws of iron. The whole of his body was burned black from the desert sun, his hair hung about him like horse's tails and his eyes blazed like coals, slit upwards in his face, while a third eye in the middle of his forehead gave out sparks of fire.

   (from *The Tale of the City Brass, The Arabian Nights*)

2 The boy swallowed the pearl. A strange burning feeling began to spread through him, from the tips of his toes to the hairs on his head. He ran to the river and drank and drank, gulping down water as fast as he could. But still he burned with the terrible fire. Then his body began to change. He grew bigger. His eyes bulged and popped. His skin became covered in golden-green scales. Horns grew from his head and wing sprouted from his back.

   (from *The Dragon Boy's Pearl* – a Chinese folk tale)

3 Now Kaliya was no ordinary serpent. He had five huge heads, with five sets of poisonous fangs, and coils so strong they could crush you to death. Soon the river was filled with Kaliya's lethal poison. Deadly fumes rose from the water which bubbled and boiled, black and sinister.

   (from *Krishna Slays the Serpent King* – an Indian folk tale)

4 Now Medusa had eagle's wings, claws of bronze, and scales instead of skin. She had two sharp bronze tusks on her face, and writhing snakes twisting and hissing instead of hair. Anyone who looked at Medusa's face was turned to stone.

   (from *Perseus and the Gorgon* – Greek Myth)

5 The Minotaur was a hideous monster, with the body of a man and the head and shoulders of a bull. It was savage and bloodthirsty, and thrived on human flesh. From deep in the Labyrinth's centre came a terrible bellowing. The ground shuddered and shook as the mighty monster stamped its feet.

   (from *Theseus and the Minotaur* – Greek Myth)

Big Writing: Six Lessons for Quick Impact © Andrell Education Ltd, 2012

LSM 7: STORY OPENERS

My	**First**
Then	**Next**
After	**Soon**
Although	**So**
However	**Meanwhile**

Big Writing: Six Lessons for Quick Impact © Andrell Education Ltd, 2012

LSM 8: CONNECTIVES

and	but
so	because
when	if
as well as	after
however	besides
even though	despite

Big Writing: Six Lessons for Quick Impact © Andrell Education Ltd, 2012

LSM 9: EXPELLED!

The Northern School of Magic

14th February 2012

Dear Herman,

What a disaster! I couldn't believe it when I heard you had been sent home! Have you really been expelled? Undoubtedly the evil Petrolous is celebrating your departure ... the malodorous little vermin!

However hard I try, I cannot believe you pushed our visitor, Sergeant Dimplemoser, down the great steps of the school. Sadly, however, so many people say they saw you do it. How can that be? Fortunately, the bushes below the path saved the Sergeant from serious injury, although his pride was badly damaged and he lost one of the stripes from his jacket.

Write soon Herman, I beg you. I know you are not a bad character and I desperately need to know what really happened. How did Sergeant Dimplemoser come to fall down the great steps?

Your loyal friend,

Harriet

LSM 10: BE THE TEACHER ...

21.03.2012

Deer Students

Thank you for the writing you did last week it was very good and I thought you did well I have assessed it all and I have gave you all a target to help you get better.

Sadly my own writing is not getting any better I am worried that I shall be sack if I don't do better soon

Your friendly teacher,

Ros. Wilson

Big Writing: Six Lessons for Quick Impact © Andrell Education Ltd, 2012

LSM 11: STORY STRUCTURE CARDS

Opening	Body
Ending	Who?
What?	Where?
When?	Why?
How?	Hopes
Fears	Feelings
Thoughts	Description

Big Writing: Six Lessons for Quick Impact © Andrell Education Ltd, 2012

LSM 12: MIST AND MOONLIGHT

Dark in the wood the shadows stir:
What do you see?
Mist and moonlight, star and cloud,
Hunchback shapes that creep and crowd
From tree to tree.

Dark in the wood a thin wind calls:
What do you hear?
Frond and fern and clutching grass
Snigger at you as you pass,
Whispering fear.

Dark in the wood a river flows:
What does it hide?
Otter, water rat, old tin can,
Bones of fish ... and bones of a man
Drift in its tide.

Dark in the wood the owlets shriek:
What do they cry?
Choose between the wood and the river;
Who comes here is lost forever,
And must die!

Raymond Wilson

Big Writing: Six Lessons for Quick Impact © Andrell Education Ltd, 2012

LSM 13: EXPLANATION LETTER

Northern School of Magic

5th June 2012

Dear Herman

What wonderful news! Everyone is thrilled to hear that you will be back with us next term. Whilst you have been excluded from NSM, we have had the opportunity to work on our individual projects for the inter-house contest. I volunteered to brief you on mine so that you can be involved in the competition after the holiday. I strongly advise you to scrutinise the following with care, in order that we may win the contest.

Explanation for 'How to Enter the Super-sonic Broomstick Flying Time Warp'

Super-sonic flight enables broomsticks to fly at considerably higher speeds and altitudes than other fliers, giving significant advantage in a range of situations. There are three main parts to entering the super-sonic time warp. These are as follows:

1. Advanced Flier Skills (AFS)

2. Favourable weather conditions

3. The super-sonic technique.

1. Advanced Flier Skills: Because the broomstick pilot has attended the AFS (Advanced Flier Skills) training school, he/she is able to manoeuvre with greater speed and precision than most. Therefore, far greater control of the broomstick is maintained while going through the techniques/motions needed to enter super-sonic flight.

2. Favourable Weather Conditions: Super-sonic flight requires a period of complete atmospheric calm, (no wind, rain or other adverse weather conditions) for the flier to pass through the Subsonic Window, (the moment of entry to super-sonic flight). Excellent weather conditions are essential for safe passage through the window. SERIOUS INCIDENTS have occurred, (mainly accidents) caused by fliers attempting to pass through the window when conditions have not been good enough.

3. The Super-sonic Flight Technique: Bare feet are essential to achieve the streamlined shape for successful passage through the window. Only highly skilful pilots of AFS status should normally fly barefooted. The broomstick is flown at an altitude of 500 meters, at a speed of 35km per hour in a southerly direction. Precision, (accuracy) is essential, with neither speed nor direction wavering. When a secure flight path is established, the pilot leans forward on the broomstick, placing the arms straight forward along the shaft with fingers touching in a point in front of the leading end of the shaft. The legs are now raised on to the broom behind, with toes pointed to stern, (the back). A rapid left and upward arm flick and shoulder lift will now whip the broomstick to the required angle and 30 degree turn which takes the broomstick through the window into super-sonic flight.

I hope you will find the above explanation useful, however I do beg you not to try it yourself, Herman, until you have done the AFS training straight after the holiday.

Your loyal friend,

Harriet

LSM 14: REPORT LETTER

Northern School of Magic

18th June 2012

Dear Herman

How COULD you? I can't believe you went against my advice and attempted a super-sonic flight! A terrible tragedy could have occurred. I enclose, below, a transcript of the report on the incident as it was published in *The Northern Times*.

Mystery Meteor Defeats Invaders

Evil invaders were defeated this morning in a dawn raid on *Carbottles* supermarket. Masked attackers swarmed in to the store on Dragon Lane and attempted to gain entrance to the warehouse at the rear, where many weeks' worth of food and drink was being stored.

The surprise attack began whilst most of the residents of North Town were still asleep. Security guards report that they had already begun the process of opening the shop for the day and were unlocking the store rooms when the invasion began. Later, an official spokesperson said that this was their usual process and that no one would have expected a goblin attack in daylight. It is being assumed that the invaders were goblins, although so far no official information has been made available.

Mystery surrounds the event which led to the defeat of the raiders. A sudden crack like thunder, and a violent flash, led to a rushing roar that swept through the deserted lane and into the warehouse at the back of *Carbottles*. All the invaders in its path were thrown to the ground, where they lay stunned until the arrival of the guards who arrested them.

This evening, representatives of the Ministry for Information reported that they were unable to explain the phenomenon that had defeated the criminals, but that everyone was very pleased that it had happened. North Town could have been without vital stores of food and drink for weeks if the daring robbery had been a success.

Of course, Herman, you are quite a hero with everyone here because they have guessed what really happened and how brave you are. For myself, I shall never speak to you again!

Yours truly,

Harriet

LSM 15: PERSUASIVE LETTER

Northern School of Magic

22nd July 2012

Dear Herman

This letter is to persuade you to rethink your decision not to apologise to the School Council. Sadly, it is not likely that you will be allowed to return to NSM unless you agree to take this simple step.

Riding a broomstick at super-sonic speeds before passing an AFS, (Advanced Flying Skills) exam is a foolish thing to do. The pilot might easily fail to get through the sonic window and the sudden loss of speed would cause him or her to stall and fall to the ground. Furthermore, evidence shows that novice riders attempting to get into position before making the sonic window manoeuvre often lose concentration and hit obstacles in their way. This is especially dangerous in built up areas like the central shopping area of North Town.

Although all pupils at NSM admire the brave action that protected their food and drink supplies, the school has rules that need to be obeyed if pupils are to develop into professional and respected witches and wizards. If all pupils disobey the rules the school will be thrown into chaos. It is certain that the Head Wizard tried to protect you by referring the matter to the School Council. However, your closest friends were unable to get to the meeting, as they were in detention for letting the hopping frogs loose in the grounds. Thus your enemies' friends were able to swing the vote against you.

There is no doubt that the Head Wizard now has no choice, and must abide by the decision of the Council. It is essential, therefore, that pride is swallowed and apologies are made. It is a small action to make in order to come back to school. If it is not done, your foul foes will have won and there will be no more Herman Clay at NSM.

Yours coolly,

Harriet

LSM 16: MY SKILL KIT

Openers from connectives

When	When I went to the shops I bought a book.
If	If I had more money I would have bought a DVD.
Although	Although I ran, I missed the bus.
Besides	Besides missing the bus, I dropped my shopping.
After	After I got home, I ate my dinner.
Before	Before I went to bed I watched some TV.
Even though	Even though it was late, I didn't feel tired.
If only	If only I had run faster, I might have got home earlier.
Despite	Despite getting up early, I was still late for school.

Openers from sequence words

First	First, I hung up my coat.
Then	Then I walked to the classroom.
Next	Next I took out my books.
After	After I took out my books I found my pencil.
Soon	Soon, the teacher started the lesson.
After a while	After a while I felt very sleepy.
Before	Before the lesson finished I fell asleep.
Meanwhile	Meanwhile, the teacher continued teaching.
When	When I woke up I didn't know what to do.
Later	Later, she had to show me how to do it.
Shortly before	Shortly before the end of the lesson, I caught up.
Shortly after	Shortly after that she collected in the books.
Finally	Finally, the lesson ended.
Eventually	Eventually, we went out to play.

Opening with –ing words, e.g.

Having eaten lunch, we went to play outside.

Walking home from school, I found a lost kitten.

Reading my book, I forgot the time.

Riding my bicycle, I got home quickly.

Big Writing: Six Lessons for Quick Impact © Andrell Education Ltd, 2012

Opening with –ly words, e.g.

Noisily, I ate my breakfast.

Happily, I ran outside to play.

Anxiously, I looked for my school book.

Excitedly, I talked to my friends.

Using punctuation for effect

Full stop .	- to end a sentence, for example: I am clever. - to show abbreviation, (shortened word) for example: Mr. Thurs. etc.
Comma ,	- to show a rest inside a sentence, for example: I am clever and beautiful, but I can't sing! - to separate items in a list, for example: I like toast, eggs, tomatoes and beans. - before speech marks or brackets, for example: I shouted, "Stop, that's mine!" It was my bike, (my new one) and I wanted it back.
Question mark ?	- at the end of a sentence that asks something, for example: Can you swim? Have you read that book?
Exclamation mark !	- at the end of a sentence that says something sharply, for example: Stop that! - at the end of a sentence that says something loud, for example: BANG! - at the end of a sentence that says something surprising or to show surprise, for example: Look, it's my bike! I've found it!
Ellipses ...	- to show something exciting, frightening or unexpected is about to happen; to create suspense, for example: I was walking along when all of a sudden ... I fell down a hole!
Speech marks "" **(inverted commas)**	- to show the words spoken by someone, for example: I said, "Go home!" She asked, "Why should I?"
Apostrophe '	- before an 's' to show that something belongs to someone or something, for example: John's books; the dog's bone. If the thing or things belong to more than one person or thing, the apostrophe goes after the s, for example: The boys' bicycles; all dogs' legs - to show that a word has been shortened by taking out one or more letters, for example: **cannot** into **can't**; **I am** into **I'm**; **we are** into **we're**
Brackets ( )	- to put in a thought or extra piece of information, for example: I have a bike, (a new one) that is red and shiny. Most of the children had arrived at the party, (wearing their fancy dress outfits) but Josh and Jenny had still not appeared.

Big Writing: Six Lessons for Quick Impact © Andrell Education Ltd, 2012

Six Quick Impact Lessons for Year 2

The Six Quick Impact Lesson Plans provided in Part Three of this book, and the accompanying Lesson Support Materials provided in Appendix 4, have been adapted by the British School, Tokyo, for use with Year 2 (and some Year 3) pupils. They are reproduced here for reference, but are intended to be adapted to suit the needs of your particular pupils.

LESSON ONE

Key objective: V=Vocabulary. To recognise and use descriptive language.

Activities	Resources
Warm Up: Introduce VCOP – Vocabulary, Connectives, Openers, Punctuation. You could use the phrase 'Very Clever Old Person' (the teacher) to help children remember VCOP. Tell children that this is something they are going to learn about that is going to help them become amazing writers. Write two sentences on the board – one which is very simple, and one which has more interesting language. Discuss why one is better, e.g. more descriptive, than the other. **Whole class activity:** Display LSM A. Identify and collect the descriptive words. **Pair activity:** Use LSM A and play 'Find the Word'. The teacher gives a word or phrase and pupils work in pairs to find the word or phrase in the text that means the same as that given.	**LSM A:** **Monsters in Stories**
Recap what has been said about interesting vocabulary in writing and how it helps to describe things more effectively. **Whole class activity:** Display and read 'Howl'. As a class, respond to the text and identify interesting vocabulary or 'WOW Words'. Brainstorm more descriptive words for monsters (use the terms 'adverb' and 'adjective'). Discuss which words are the most effective and why. **Independent writing (20 mins):** Children write the next paragraph to continue the 'Howl' story. They can use the descriptive words collected and/or their own WOW words in their writing. Focus on using these words for effect. Stop after 10 minutes and ask how many WOW Words they have used so far. Praise and continue for 10 more minutes. **Basic Skills Check:** Ask pupils to check their work for full stops and capital letters, correct spellings and neat handwriting. **Plenary:** Review learning on Vocabulary and the purpose of descriptive words. *Display the WOW words collected in the teaching space and add to them often.*	**LSM B:** **Howl**

Big Writing: Six Lessons for Quick Impact in Year 2© Andrell Education Ltd, 2012

LESSON TWO

Key objective: C=Connectives. To recognise and use a range of connectives.

Activities	Resources
Warm Up: Recap VCOP – Vocabulary, Connectives, Openers, Punctuation. You could use the phrase 'Very Clever Old Person' (the teacher) to help children remember VCOP. Ask/help children to think of a range of connecting words, e.g. and, but, so, then. Record these and discuss how these words are used to structure sentences by connecting ideas and/or showing the passage of time. **Pair activity:** Use LSM 8 *(see Appendix 4)* and ask children to make up sentences using some of the simpler connectives. Children should scribe their best sentence on to a mini whiteboard or similar. Share the sentences as a class. Discuss how you might change the sentence by moving the connective to the beginning. What is the impact on the sentence of using the connective as an opener? **Pair activity:** Display LSM C and play 'Spot the Difference' using the two extracts. What makes the second extract a higher level than the first? Note the use of a range of interesting connectives.	**LSM 8: Connectives** *(See Appendix 4)* **LSM C: Snow White in the City**
Recap what has been said about using connectives in writing. **Whole class activity:** Display LSM C and ask pupils to come up and highlight the connectives used in the second extract. **Independent writing (20 mins):** Give children the connective cards. Using LSM D as a starting point, children continue the story of 'Snow White in the City' including connectives to link ideas in their writing. Stop after 10 minutes and ask how many Connectives they have used so far. Praise and continue for 10 more minutes. **Basic Skills Check:** Ask pupils to check their work for full stops and capital letters, correct spellings and neat handwriting. **Plenary:** Review learning on Connectives by playing oral sentence games. *Display the Connectives collected in the teaching space.*	**LSM 8: Connectives** *(See Appendix 4)* **LSM D: Snow White in the City**

Big Writing: Six Lessons for Quick Impact in Year 2© Andrell Education Ltd, 2012

LESSON THREE

Key objective: O=Openers. To recognise and use a range of openers.

Activities	Resources
Warm Up: Recap VCOP – Vocabulary, Connectives, Openers, Punctuation. You could use the phrase 'Very Clever Old Person' (the teacher) to help children remember VCOP. Ask/help children to think of sentence opening words, e.g. My, Then, Next, Soon, However. Record these and discuss how these words are used to grab the reader's attention. Do some quick-fire oral work – "Make me up a sentence beginning with …" using a range of openers. "Who can think of a better word to open this sentence, to make it a higher level?" **Whole class activity:** Display a child's piece of work (anonymous) or a piece from the Imaginary Friend. Read it together and identify the aspects of VCOP, especially the sentence openers used. **Pair activity:** Display LSM C and play 'Spot the Difference' using the two extracts. What makes the second extract a higher level than the first? Note the use of a range of interesting connectives.	**LSM 7:** **Story openers** *(See Appendix 4)*
Recap what has been said about using openers in writing. **Pair activity:** Give children LSM E and ask children to identify and highlight the openers, then work with a partner to change and improve them. **Independent writing (20 mins):** Children write a reply to the letter, as if they were Katie, explaining how they got Woolly the sheep out of the Boggy Loch. Encourage them to focus on use of interesting openers. Can they use connectives as openers? Give them LSM 7 for support. Stop after 10 minutes and ask how many different openers children have used. Has anyone used a connective to open a sentence? Praise and continue for 10 more minutes. **Basic Skills Check:** Ask pupils to check their work for full stops and capital letters, correct spellings and neat handwriting. **Plenary:** Review learning on Openers by playing oral sentence games. *Display the Openers collected in the teaching space.*	**LSM E:** **Letter from Grannie** **LSM 7:** **Story openers** *(See Appendix 4)*

Big Writing: Six Lessons for Quick Impact in Year 2© Andrell Education Ltd, 2012

LESSON FOUR

Key objective: P=Punctuation. To recognise and use a range of punctuation.

Activities	Resources
Warm Up: Recap VCOP – Vocabulary, Connectives, Openers, Punctuation. You could use the phrase 'Very Clever Old Person' (the teacher) to help children remember VCOP. Ask/help children to think of different types of punctuation. Record these and discuss how each piece of punctuation is used. Ask children to come up and illustrate with examples.	**The Punctuation Pyramid** *(See Appendix 2)*
Whole class activity: Introduce the Punctuation Pyramid and discuss how it represents progression in use of punctuation, from very basic through to more sophisticated. Name all of the punctuation. Write two sentences up on the board and ask children, working with partners, to rewrite them at a higher standard using the Pyramid to help.	**LSM F: Punctuation for effect**
Pair activity: Using LSM F children can play 'Spot the Difference'. What makes the second extract a higher standard than the first? Ask pupils to identify and name all the pieces of punctuation in the second piece. What else makes the second piece a higher standard? Look at the range of vocabulary, connectives and openers.	
Recap what has been said about using punctuation in writing.	**LSM G: The Monster**
Whole class activity: Display and read 'The Monster'. Discuss what pupils like and dislike about this piece. Is it an effective description? Why or why not?	**The Punctuation Pyramid** *(See Appendix 2)*
Pair activity: Give pupils a copy of LSM G and ask them to identify the different types of punctuation. (More able children could identify other aspects of VCOP.)	
Independent writing (20 mins): Children write the next paragraph to continue the story of 'The Monster'. Encourage them to focus on using different types of punctuation for effect. Stop after 10 minutes and ask how many types of punctuation children have used. Has anyone used an interesting connective or opener? Has anyone used any WOW words? Praise and continue for 10 more minutes.	
Basic Skills Check: Ask pupils to check their work for full stops and capital letters, correct spellings and neat handwriting.	
Plenary: Review learning on Punctuation by playing a game with the Punctuation Pyramid.	
Display the Punctuation Pyramid in the teaching space.	

LESSON FIVE

Key objective: To find and use features of good writing.

Activities	Resources
Warm Up: Recap VCOP – Vocabulary, Connectives, Openers, Punctuation. Do some quick-fire oral activities, for example: • Who can make me up a sentence with (choose opener)? • Who can use (choose connective) in a sentence? • Which punctuation would go in this sentence? • How many WOW words are there in this sentence? **Whole class activity:** Look at the Sensational Sentences on LSM H (or scribe up sentences from pupils' work). Why are these sentences sensational? Identify VCOP features. **Pair activity:** Hand out LSM I. Explain that Katie has written a letter to the class telling us about her Uncle Pete's sheep. She needs some help to improve it using VCOP! Working in pairs pupils edit and improve Katie's letter. Less able could simply insert the new features; more able can write the new text on the line below.	**LSM H: Sensational Sentences** **LSM I: Katie's letter**
Recap what has been said about using VCOP in writing. **Whole class activity:** Tell pupils they are going to write a reply to Katie's letter. Display it again and discuss ideas. What kind of things will you write? Can we describe where we live? How is it different? What things do we enjoy doing? In pairs, pupils could orally rehearse some sentences. You could ask different pairs to focus on different aspects of VCOP. **Independent writing (20 mins):** Children write their letters to Katie, using all aspects of VCOP to write at their best level. Stop after 10 minutes and ask how many VCOP features children have used. Has anyone used an interesting connective or opener? Has anyone used any WOW words? Praise and continue for 10 more minutes. **Basic Skills Check:** Ask pupils to check their work for full stops and capital letters, correct spellings and neat handwriting.	**LSM I: Katie's letter**

LESSON SIX

Key objective: To find and use features of good writing.

Activities	Resources
Warm Up: Recap VCOP – Vocabulary, Connectives, Openers, Punctuation. Do some quick-fire oral activities, for example: • Who can make me up a sentence with (choose opener)? • Who can use (choose connective) in a sentence? • Which punctuation would go in this sentence? • How many WOW words are there in this sentence? **Whole class activity:** Look at the letter on LSM J. Identify and highlight aspects of VCOP. Different pairs or groups of children could focus on different aspects of VCOP. **Pair activity:** Give children some simple sentences and ask them to 'up-level' the sentences using VCOP. You could use some of the sentences on LSM H. **Independent writing (20 mins):** Children write a letter back to Nelly, using all aspects of VCOP to write at their best level. Stop after 10 minutes and ask how many VCOP features children have used. Has anyone used an interesting connective or opener? Has anyone used any WOW words? Praise and continue for 10 more minutes. **Basic Skills Check:** Ask pupils to check their work for accurate punctuation, correct spellings and neat handwriting.	**LSM J:** **Nelly's Letter** **LSM H:** **Sensational Sentences** **(Optional)**

Big Writing: Six Lessons for Quick Impact in Year 2© Andrell Education Ltd, 2012

LSM A: MONSTERS IN STORIES

The minotaur was a hideous monster, with the body of a man and the head of a cow. It was bloodthirsty and liked eating humans! From deep in the Labyrinth came a terrible bellowing. The ground shook as the mighty monster stamped its feet.

(Theseus and the Minotaur, Greek myth)

Kailua was a terrible serpent. He had five huge heads with five sets of poisonous teeth. His body was so strong that he could crush you to death. Soon the river was filled with Kaliya's poison. Deadly smoke came up from the water which bubbled and boiled, black and spooky.

(Krishna and the Serpent King, Indian Traditional tale)

The scary monster was green and smelly. Blood dripped out of his mouth as he roared and screamed. His skin was slimy and bumpy with big red blotches. As he came out of his cave, the earth shook.

Big Writing: Six Lessons for Quick Impact in Year 2© Andrell Education Ltd, 2012

LSM B: HOWL

Who would have thought such small creatures could have made so much noise? Bravely, I carried on, clearing a way through all the tiny people as they made their way to the temple.

"Go back!" they said. "Go back before it is too late!" But I carried on into the gloomy night. I had to complete my mission.

Strangely, the inside seemed quiet after the panic of outside. I stood quietly, listening carefully for a sound. All was quiet … too quiet! I waited.

After what seemed like a long time, I crept forward and moved between the chairs and books all over the floor. I didn't make a single sound as I floated towards the tomb at the back of the temple. My hand was resting on the big, cold handle of the door when the crazy, blood-chilling scream ripped through the air. It was the cry of death....

_____

_____

_____

_____

_____

_____

_____

_____

LSM C: SNOW WHITE IN THE CITY

Once upon a time in New York there was a poor, little, rich girl called Snow White. Her mother was dead. For a while she lived happily with her father. Then one day he married again. All the papers said that Snow White's stepmother was the classiest dame in New York. No one knew that she was the Queen of the Underworld. She liked to see herself in the New York Mirror. One day she read something that made her very jealous:
'Snow White—the belle of New York City'.
She plotted to get rid of her stepdaughter.

Once upon a time in the city of New York there lived a poor, little, rich girl called Snow White. Snow White's mother had died some years ago and for a time she lived happily with her father. Her father was a kind and generous man. Often he would come home with toys and books for her. Sometimes he would bring beautiful clothes and shoes and she would dance with delight.

Then Snow White's father told her that he was going to marry again. To everyone else, Snow White's stepmother was the classiest dame in New York but Snow White knew that she was really very cruel and mean. She liked to gaze at herself in the mirror because she believed she was the most beautiful woman in the whole world. Then, one day, she read a newspaper headline: 'Snow White – the Belle of New York City'. She was horrified that someone else might be more beautiful, so she vowed to get rid of her stepdaughter.

Big Writing: Six Lessons for Quick Impact in Year 2© Andrell Education Ltd, 2012

LSM D: SNOW WHITE IN THE CITY

Once upon a time in the city of New York there lived a poor little rich girl called Snow White. Snow White's mother had died some years ago and for a time she lived happily with her father. Her father was a kind and generous man. Often he would come home with toys and books for her. Sometimes he would bring beautiful clothes and shoes and she would dance with delight.

Then Snow White's father told her that he was going to marry again. To everyone else, Snow White's stepmother was the classiest dame in New York but Snow White knew that she was really very cruel and mean. She liked to gaze at herself in the mirror because she believed she was the most beautiful woman in the whole world. Then, one day, she read a newspaper headline: 'Snow White – the Belle of New York City'. She was horrified that someone else might be more beautiful so she vowed to get rid of her stepdaughter.

_____

_____

_____

_____

_____

_____

_____

Big Writing: Six Lessons for Quick Impact in Year 2© Andrell Education Ltd, 2012

LSM E: LETTER FROM GRANNIE

**Haggis Cottage
Scotland**

Dear Katie,

What a disaster! I heard that Uncle Pete's sheep, Woolly, got stuck in the Boggy Loch again! How did this happen? I'm sure Uncle Pete must be furious with her...the mischievous sheep!

When I spoke to your mother on the telephone, she told me that you helped Uncle Pete get Woolly out of the loch. Sadly, she didn't have time to tell me how you managed to do this. Was it difficult? What did you use to help you? Of course, I hope that Woolly was not hurt at all. She really is the most beautiful, elegant sheep on the Isle of Coll.

Write soon Katie, I so look forward to hearing from you. I really would like to know how you and Uncle Pete got Woolly out of that muddy, soggy loch.

Lots of Love,

Grannie

Big Writing: Six Lessons for Quick Impact in Year 2© Andrell Education Ltd, 2012

LSM F: PUNCTUATION FOR EFFECT

A man walked down the castle steps. He walked towards the forest as if he did not want to be seen. Sam recognised him. It was Mr Foster. Where was he going?

A hooded figure came swiftly down the front steps of the castle. After reaching the bottom, he walked as quickly as possible towards the Forbidden Forest. Harry recognised the man's prowling walk ... Mr Foster! Snatching a quick look behind, Mr Foster disppeared into the trees. What was going on?

Big Writing: Six Lessons for Quick Impact in Year 2© Andrell Education Ltd, 2012

LSM G: THE MONSTER

With fear, I padded carefully down the dark, damp tunnel. My hands were shaking, so I put them in my pockets. I could see and hear nothing ... nothing but the sound of my own panicked breathing. Suddenly an evil smell crept up my nose, like the rotting smell of meat. I stopped, my heart pounding. Was there something in the inky darkness? Before I became even more terrified, I pulled out my torch and shone it up the tunnel. Silence surrounded me but then ... out of the blackness came a terrifying shriek!

_____

_____

_____

_____

_____

_____

_____

Big Writing: Six Lessons for Quick Impact in Year 2© Andrell Education Ltd, 2012

LSM H: SENSATIONAL SENTENCES

1. Uncle Pete is irate because Woolly the sheep has been terribly naughty.

2. First, we got a ladder but it didn't work.

3. Meanwhile, while you were at the show, we went to the shops.

4. Before very long we had hoisted Woolly out of the clutches of the Boggy Loch.

5. I will tell you all about Grannie's glittering, beautiful ring.

6. Finally, Woolly began to swim towards us and we scrambled to the water's edge to grab her. She was free!

Big Writing: Six Lessons for Quick Impact in Year 2© Andrell Education Ltd, 2012

LSM I: KATIE'S LETTER

The Post Office
Isle of Coll

Dear Friends

My name is Katie and I live on an island in Scotland.

I like painting and swimming in the loch.

It is nice here. My family all live close by.

My Uncle Pete has a naughty sheep. She is called Woolly.

Yesterday we had to get her out of the Boggy Loch.

It was hard work. We needed three people and a big rope.

We all got muddy.

Then we went back to Uncle Pete's house for hot chocolate.

Please write and tell me about your life.

Love from Katie

Big Writing: Six Lessons for Quick Impact in Year 2© Andrell Education Ltd, 2012

LSM J: NELLY'S LETTER

House 2
The Village

Dear Grace

First, I would like to say how much I enjoyed your visit to the

village this weekend. Although the weather was stormy, I still had a

fascinating time with you and so enjoyed our supper by the fire! Even

though it is a lot to ask, I would like you to visit our beautiful village

again next weekend because ... I have something incredibly important

to ask you! After you have decided if you can come, could you send

me a letter to let me know?

All my Love,

Nelly

Big Writing: Six Lessons for Quick Impact in Year 2© Andrell Education Ltd, 2012

An Eight Week Impact Strategy

Raising Standards in Year 6

This model is designed for teachers who first meet *Big Writing* towards the end of Year 6, and who face the urgent challenge of raising standards for pupils about to complete their primary education. It is still possible to make an impact on standards within an eight-week timescale through the following intervention.

You will need:

- Loads of energy (essential).
- Support to make the resources (desirable).
- Money to buy special portfolios and pens (desirable).
- A Mozart track and CD/music player (essential).
- A way to dim the classroom lighting (essential).
- A lava lamp or large candle held firmly in a tin holder (essential).
- Edible 'goals' as rewards, e.g. grapes, orange segments or sweets (essential).
- Enthusiasm, commitment, belief and perseverance (essential).

The Big Write time prompts

During the 45 minute silent writing session the teacher gives the Time Prompts shown on pages 25-26. These serve the purpose of reminding children what they need to achieve in their writing, and also provide valuable 'brain breaks'.

The VCOP chant as a hook

'Hooks' are strategies for enabling pupils to quickly re-access prior learning. They may be slogans, acronyms, mnemonics, catch phrases, rhymes, chants or similar.

In *Big Writing* we recommend that pupils are always required to write at their 'best level'. Consistent use of the VCOP chant below has proved to be a highly effective hook for pupils in helping them to achieve 'best level' in all writing opportunities.

"What have we got to remember? The **VCOP**!"

The chant is done as a visual, auditory and kinaesthetic activity. Pupils use both hands to make a V shape as they say 'V', the left hand to make a C shape as they say 'C', both hands to make the O as they say 'O' and both hands to make a P shape as they say 'P'. Adults modelling need to remember to reverse the P and C shapes so that they are visually correct for the children watching.

Once a week for five weeks	**Weekly *Big Writing* lesson** **Duration:** one and a half hours – two 45 minute sessions with morning playtime in the middle. Use the VCOP chant at the start of the lesson. **Session 1:** • 35 minutes – series of fast, fun, oral activities around VCOP • 10 minutes – time to jot ideas down, pupils choose how to plan **Session 2:** The 'Big Write' – pupils write in silence for 45 minutes; softened lighting, candle/lava lamp, Mozart music on low volume. Pupils have A4 lined paper with a margin, and special pens on the desks. Change the text type every week. Use time prompts to ensure use of VCOP
Days leading up to *Big Writing* lesson	**Stocking Fillers** Frequent, fast, fun activities on VCOP, for example: • A few minutes of quick-fire 'Who can make me up …?' • Longer (10-15 minute) up-levelling activities, using the work of the 'imaginary friend'.
The afternoon before the *Big Writing* session	15 minutes: As late as possible in the day, introduce the stimulus for the 'Big Write' session the following day, and the text type to be used. Show and remind pupils the characteristics of the text type and discuss the stimulus. Set a 'Talk Homework'.
Day after the *Big Writing* session	**Celebration of Success/Goal Scorers** 10-15 minutes at any point of the day in which pupils can: • Highlight good examples of VCOP in their own and/or a partner's writing. • Compare two pieces of writing – play 'Spot the Difference'. • Compare the three pieces of writing from that week. Are all at the same high level for both the WHATs and the HOWs? • Improve or 'up-level' their writing.
Additional writing session/s	• Writing in another subject and using a different text type, e.g. a persuasive letter about an environmental issue, a history report, an explanation for science. • Time taken from 'subject time' not English. • Use the VCOP chant before pupils start writing. • Prepare in a previous lesson in that subject and review the stimulus and text type before the writing session, as above. • In the writing session, dim the lights, use a lava lamp or candle and play Mozart. • Pupils write for 45 minutes. Cover one further text type each week in another subject under 'Big Write' conditions as above. This could be another extended writing session or a shorter piece.
Once a week for the final three weeks	Change the structure of the *Big Writing* session to: **Session 1:** 35 minutes of fast, fun, oral VCOP activities **Session 2:** Sample 'test' conditions, writing to a previously unseen task for 50-55 minutes. Retain the 'Big Write' atmosphere for this session.

Julie Horsington was a newly qualified teacher in Year 6 at Southern Road Primary School.

Southern Road Primary School is a large, four form entry primary school in the Plaistow area of the London Borough of Newham. The number on role at the time of writing (2005) was 868 of whom 68% had English as an additional language, (EAL).13% had special educational needs and over 50% were entitled to free school meals. There had been a dramatic rise in mobility in the academic years 2003/04 and 2004/05.

Julie wrote:

"I first thought of Kung Fu punctuation when the literacy consultant for Newham, Pam. Clarke, came into my classroom to teach the 6 'quick impact' lessons from Ros. Wilson's book.

Although my pupils were only taught from this remarkable programme for a brief time period, the improvements made in their writing were astonishing. Not only did this programme raise standards in pupils' skills and writing but it also raised enthusiasm levels in my class due to the fun, stimulating nature of the activities Ros. has developed.

The development of Kung Fu punctuation really came from the pupils themselves. The energy and enthusiasm they displayed really carried this activity to the next level. This idea was a development from one of Ros.'s activities and is all about promoting the idea of learning being fun."

INSTRUCTIONS FOR PUNCTUATION KUNG FU

1 Refer to the Punctuation Pyramid on display in the classroom and review which punctuation marks the children should be using for their target levels.

2 Teach the children the physical actions for the punctuation signs, (see opposite).

3 Read out the first prepared sentence, e.g. Although Kathy knew that it was cheating, she could not help taking a peep.

4 Give the children 10 seconds thinking time to work out the punctuation for each sentence.

5 The teacher says, "First punctuation mark!"

6 Children respond, "HUH!" as they perform the action for a capital letter.

7 Teacher says, "Second punctuation mark!"

8 Children respond, "HUH!" as they perform the action for a comma. If the punctuation mark has two movements, as in an exclamation mark, children must say, "HUH! HUH!" as they perform the two movements.

9 Teacher says, "Third punctuation mark!"

10 Children respond "HUH!" as they perform the action for a full stop.

11 Briefly discuss any elements of usage felt necessary before going on to the next sentence.

THE PHYSICAL ACTIONS

NB EACH MOVEMENT MUST BE ACCOMPANIED BY A GUTTERAL "HUH!" AS IN THE SPORT, KUNG FU.

ALL PUPILS SHOULD STAND AND FACE THE TEACHER.

1 CAPITAL LETTER
Both hands above head, finger tips together and thumbs touching to form capital A shape.

2 FULL STOP.
Punch air forwards once, horizontally.

3 QUESTION MARK?
Right hand raised to make comma shape, left fist punches once
sideways below.

4 EXCLAMATION MARK!
Right arm raised high, then dropped. Left fist punches once sideways below.

5 COMMA,
Right elbow at waist, with forearm pointing upwards, make 'hook'
or comma shape at the top with
right hand.

6 ELLIPSES ...
horizontal forward punches

7 SPEECH MARKS ""
Arms raised, both hands form '' to top left of body and then rapidly again to top right.

8 DASH -
Horizontal karate chop sideways with right hand, which is open and flat with palm downwards.

9 APOSTROPHE'
Arm raised to form comma shape in the air above the head.

10 COLON:
2 horizontal punches forward, first one above the second one.

11 SEMI COLON;
Right hand makes comma shape at chest height, left hand punches horizontally and sideways above it.

12 BRACKETS ()
Big curved shape with left arm extended upwards to left of head, followed by big curved shape with right arm extended upwards to right of head.

EXAMPLES OF SENTENCES USED WITH JULIE'S CLASS
1   This is a pencil.
2   Where is my phone?
3   Come here at once!
4   Have you seen my keys?
5   Harry woke up early the next morning.
6   Although he could tell it was daylight, he kept his eyes shut.
7   All of a sudden….
8   That's outrageous!
9   The sky was quite clear now and the sea gleamed in
     the sunlight.
10 Hagrid's coat seemed to be made of nothing but pockets,
     bunches of keys, slug pellets, balls of string, mint humbugs
     and tea bags.

An Additional Adaptation to Kung Fu Punctuation by the writer.
All pupils stand facing teacher with feet approximately 45 cms
apart. They bend their knees slightly.
Pupils give TWO 'HUHs' for each piece of punctuation:

HUH 1: Small jump with bent knees
Right arm in front of chest bent at elbow with forearm pointing
upwards, fingers together and pointed upwards.
Left arm bent at elbow across chest beyond right arm, fingers
together and pointing horizontally.

HUH 2: Second small jump with bent knees. One or both arms
making sign for punctuation as above.

There will be 3 'HUHs' if the piece of punctuation has 2 Moves.
*Each time they shout "HUH!" for any movement they actually make
a small jump with bent knees.*